SEPARATE LIFETIMES

"We who choose to surround ourselves with lives even more temporary than our own live within a fragile circle, easily and often breached. Unable to accept its awful gaps, we still would live no other way. We cherish memory as the only certain immortality, never fully understanding the necessary plan."

from *The Once Again Prince*

SEPARATE LIFETIMES

by IRVING TOWNSEND

J. N. TOWNSEND PUBLISHING

TIVOLI, NEW YORK

Copyright © 1986 J. N. Townsend Publishing

Published by
J. N. Townsend Publishing
Box 8
Tivoli, New York 12583

Grateful acknowledgment is made to the following publications in which these essays first appeared: "How to Spend A Two-Dog Night": *Harper's Magazine*. "Peacocks! Help!," "Homecoming and Going," "A Trip to the City," "The Fur That Flies," "Anniversary," "A Morning Walk with Darwin," "The Fouth Cat": *The Country Journal*. "The Private Life of the Final Flower," "At the Death of an Oak," "The Once Again Prince": *Reader's Digest*. "The Watch Cat": *Ladies' Home Journal*.

Book design by Martha E. Raines

Cover art & Illustrations by Judith Roberts-Rondeau

Printed in the United States of America

Library of Congress Cataloging-in-Publication Data

Townsend, Irving.
  Separate lifetimes
  1. Country life—United States.   2. Nature
3. Animals—Anecdotes.   I. Title.
S521.5.A2T69   1986   508.73   86-24964
ISBN 0-9617426-0-7

♦ —————————— In publishing this book, many individuals deserve acknowledgment for their unlimited encouragement, confidence, and sacrifice, which brought SEPARATE LIFETIMES to life.

To Martha E. Raines, Judith Roberts-Rondeau, and Susan Merritt: your talents have produced a beautiful book, and your spirits have continually boosted mine. To my mother, Freddie Townsend, a great deal of love, respect, and gratitude is owed for her unconditional support and her long-distance nurturing. To Jo and Alfred Hart, Bill and Beth Robbins, and all of the author's devoted friends, my thanks for your advice, ideas, assistance, and perseverance. Very special thanks go to Joseph Moody for his exceptional patience during this obsession, and to my very own "family of animals."

—J. N. Townsend

Essays

Anniversary	9
The Watch Cat	15
The Last Roundup	23
My Son, The Colt	29
A Walk into Spring	33
Mourning Becomes a Dove	37
At the Death of An Oak	41
The Visitor	45
April Eyes are Wider Eyes	51
We Can't All Be Cats	55
How to Spend a Two-Dog Night	59
Continuity of Collies	63
Homecoming and Going	67
A Prisoner in A Game Bird Sanctuary	79

The Noninterruptibles	87
The Spirit of May is Blithe	93
Immortal Hari	97
In Other Words	109
A Morning Walk with Darwin	117
The Private Life of the Final Flower	125
Peacocks! Help!	129
The Starling Rodeo	137
The Fur That Flies	141
The Fourth Cat	149
The Lake That Burps	157
Wouldn't You Rather Be Purple?	163
The Once Again Prince	167

◆――――――◆

For Elodio

Anniversary

October, the month of pumpkin moons and stubble fields, where the colors of autumn are old green and gold and the only splash of new red paint is the patch of poison oak, is an anniversary month for me. It was on an October day that I found this valley and knew it suited me, and, although I have often seen it better dressed since then, the muted patterns of October remind me of that day. Like all anniversaries, an October day is overlaid for me with bright memories and so becomes more vivid than it really is.

I arrived reluctantly in Southern California, the first twig on my small branch of the family tree ever to venture west of the Berkshires and at a point in my life when I felt neither the extra push Emerson ascribed to the young, nor the need of the old for a more benign climate. I had been sent to become my company's man in Hollywood and had traded my Connecticut farm for a glass house in a West Los Angeles suburb. Until my arrival in the west the summers of my life had been spent along the New England coast, the Octobers commuting between country and city. My father was a country man by birth and inclination whose heart was with the fishermen he knew from Cape Porpoise, Maine, to Martha's Vineyard. I grew up eating chowder suppers at round, oil-cloth-covered kitchen tables, listening to stories of the sea, leaving early but never empty handed. There would be a mess of wild blueberries for my mother, a bucket of bait for my father, and the silent promise to ourselves that one day we would return to stay. The smell of the sea, the creak of an oarlock at dawn, the eel ponds and cranberry bogs, the early autumns and deep winters of New England suited me fine. Until I was forty years old the western sky held the promise of tomorrow's weather. I never thought of the land it covered.

It was these visits to the sea, the rest of the year divided between a city job and a country home, which taught me the blessings of a small community. But that was New England country, often harsh, never submissive. The unpredictable habits of sea creatures, the good and bad fruit years, the effort required to accomplish even small tasks seemed the only way of life. We followed our friends to sea and to church and the morning's catch in both was usually worth the trip. When the fish traps were hauled up empty, the nets torn by invading shark, defeat was accepted. "Some say He sends in the shark to keep us from takn' too many," my father's fisherman crony told me as we headed home with an empty hold. When we met again outside the country church after service, the faces of the fishermen weathered below the eyes, their foreheads dead white from the protecting visors of their caps, my father's friend would smile. "Never changes a word, our preacher, but we keep a-comin' anyway."

Then I was under western skies, condemned to paradise and a year without seasons, to a land of adjacent suburbs, neither self-governed nor self-sufficient. I set out in desperation to search for something within driving distance of Hollywood more compatible with my memories of maples and meadows and the stone fences of my Connecticut farm.

North of Los Angeles the settlements are smaller, their Spanish names taken from early Spanish missions — Ventura, Santa Barbara, Santa Ynez — adobe fortresses of Christian faith which once stood alone in savage country, each of them younger than my Connecticut farmhouse. The cities lie low between the mountains and the sea, their flat rooftops squeezed under the tufts of palm trees, their presence as temporary as the trailer parks they resemble. Only the mission-style courthouses and ancient haciendas seem permanent. Wherever mountainside and highway touch, signs warn of falling rocks, as if the western edge of the continent had yet to settle its boundary.

I turned inland over coastal mountains, driving through a national forest which that October was a tangle of greasewood brush without a visible tree. Ahead stretched an inland valley bright gold that morning, its shorn fields dotted with cattle, its knolls wearing boutonnieres of bottle-green live oaks. The smell of autumn rose around me, the dead, dry aroma of old grasses. Gone was the tropic vegetation of the southern coast, the citrus groves and caressing temperatures. Instead, walnut orchards stood ready for harvest and smoke plumes rose from ranch-house chimneys. A country town circled a white church spire, its old houses half buried in the yellow foliage of cottonwoods. A river bed, dry and ready for action, wound along the edge of the town. It was not quite New England, but it was close to it.

The ranch I bought is small by local standards, smaller than the farm I left in Connecticut, but privacy here is not defined by fence lines, and there is not a house in sight. Its circle of trees includes California natives, Monterey pine and live oak, imported dazzlers, liquid amber and ornamental fruit trees, and old friends, silver birch and sycamore. Morning frost dusts the shingles of my roof between October and April, and an oval of black ice covers the horse trough on winter mornings. Two hours from Hollywood I had found seasons only slightly modified from those I remembered. Better still, I had found small communities proud of their pasts, surrounded by open country unlikely to be subdivided because this valley could not serve as a bedroom. It was too far from the kitchen.

I live between two small towns, each settled less than a century ago, their populations hardly larger today than they were in 1890. And because little more than a century separates today's Californians from its pilgrims, even the oldest residents were usually born somewhere else. One of my first visits was to a woman older than her town. "I walked across those mountains to get here," she told me, "driving six cows in front of me." She gave me a bag of walnuts to take home. I was told about another early settler in the valley north of this one. Midway across the continent her husband had refused to go on, she to return. They sawed their wagon in two, divided their horses, and the woman arrived in California alone in half a wagon.

The newer-comers, those who settled in this century, speak in accents of the south- and middlewest, of Mexico and occasionally of New England, but all have come to stay, and their common interests and common pride in this place bind them together. The single force, I believe, which turns country strangers into country friends and allies is the weather. It affects us all, our forecasts are as good as the next man's, our hopes shared. It is the conversation opener on every country morning; it turns us into natives, introduces us to our neighbors, and equalizes us more effectively than the Constitution.

Not long after I arrived here I met a man born as I was in Springfield, Massachusetts, and, like me, a recent settler. "Would you go back if you could?" he asked me. I had to think before I answered. I was no longer bound to Hollywood. I could return to New England, perhaps, to live as my father and I once planned to live long ago. But long absence separated me from home and the threads that bound me were being broken as old friends wrote less frequently, only to tell me I wouldn't know the places I remembered. "Perhaps to visit," I finally answered. "Would you?" He shook his head. "I don't see why we need to," he said.

And we really don't. I am surrounded now by new geography. The sea is to the west, and the western sky does seem bigger, if only because there is so little in the way of it. In a single year we have experienced fire, flood and earthquake within a few miles of my house, and once again October finds us thirsty. But the country works its wonders everywhere. While cities and nations are born out of economic and political necessity and a community of nations is self contradictory, the country town is a natural expression of our humanity wherever it occurs.

I have not come so far as I once thought, and even the sea is only a mountain away. Every now and then, when the wind is right, we get a whiff of it, a smell which reminds a friend of mine of fresh-cut watermelon. Not bad for an October morning.

Joseph Wood Krutch, another transplanted New Englander, wrote, "When men lived most intimately with things which were alive they thought of themselves as living."

I feel that way today. Happy Anniversary!

The Watch Cat

He is not my cat. The crisis which for a while made me his man nearly destroyed our friendship, bending our lives until they bumped. We were never meant to know each other well, never certainly to endure the false intimacy of nurse and patient, the cat-box relationship so unnecessary where a country cat and country man live side by side. Before the shot was fired I could be called a friend of the family, a familiar face. I had met his grandmother, which is more than he can say, and I recognized on him her formal dress of basic black, charcoal shadowed in bright sunlight. He had also inherited her shirtfront and the random splashes of white across her legs. She had carried her first family to the woodpile inside a fenced enclosure on the east side of my garage, a safe house for cats on the run. Tucked between oak logs, her kittens practiced their amazing graces, learned bluff from blunder and discovered what fun it is to be a cat.

His mother was quiet and wild and she never trusted me. He was born between hay bales in the stable where she never thought I would look, and not until his eyes were open did she move him and his siblings to the woodpile. By then I had acknowledged a permanence of cats in my immediate circle and was providing a pan filled with canned and dry cat food to a dozen feline visitors each morning. He was the first of his generation to climb to the topping board, then to the connecting branch leading to the roof of my house. It was there that he took up his watch at the roof edge, waiting for me, then following along above me to breakfast.

His was the first cat face I saw each morning, and for many weeks I saw only his face, floating along the shingled rim of my house, appearing through the branches of his climbing tree, finally rising above the fence as he waited for me to catch up with breakfast. Even his kitten face was startling. His eyes were larger than the other cats' eyes and the color of pharoah's gold. A scattering of eyebrow rose above them to form a high tiara spiked and frosted. His male face was broad, but flaring tufts extended it and long whiskers swept to either side. His stare was owlishly angry, point blank and fearless. I was always the first to look away.

He was still an adolescent when he came down from his catwalk to meet me at my door. Three dogs precede me through that door, tumbling into morning to chase night scents, spreading early birds and careless cats before them. But not the watch cat, as I had come to call him. He stood his ground as determinedly as a surfer meets a wave, then walked ahead of me to the enclosure, tail stiff, ears flattened against the breath of dogs. Inside, his sisters and brothers waited out of sight until the door was closed before they ventured to the pan. Not the watch cat. He settled to his meal without a backward glance. And as my wild cat family grew and tiptoed into a wider world, the watch cat went his way alone to see what else there was beyond the safe circle of trees.

He spent his first summer prowling the pasture, freezing above a gopher hole, zigzagging among the cattle, dozing on the roof in early afternoons. We met occasionally, and then he joined me, his stride always more purposeful than mine. He seemed to need to reach my destination first, then go on a little farther to his own. His watch on the world continued. He took up vigil along the ridge line of my roof where he sat within his tail beside the weather vane, watching. He patrolled the fence lines, impelled by more than appetite and instinct justified. Food and females, after all, were nearer home. His was a total freedom because he used it without limit. If he had been born a man he would have discovered a lost continent or been first to reach a star. I understood this, and, while I felt the satisfaction a parent takes in the accomplishments of an exceptional child, I envied him. We like to see ourselves as syntheses of all in nature we admire, a sum greater than its parts. We call ourselves tigers and eagles, hawks and doves; we are foxy, bullish and dogged. We work like beavers, run like deer and are wise as owls. Most often, however, we see ourselves as cats. Watching the watch cat on his rounds reminded me of the gap which forever separates us from the qualities we so admire and would assume. He seemed to burn a little brighter than the rest of us, and he always made it look so easy.

A week of heavy rain in the closing days of January was celebrated by men, not cats. In such weather the outdoor cats retreat to rafters, to empty stalls, but they appear even in a downpour at the breakfast pan. For the first three days of that rainy week the watch cat was missing. I was not concerned; he had taken overnight trips before, and the rain had driven gophers from their flooded bedrooms. There was food enough without my offering. The climax of the storm came early Thursday morning, bringing rain so heavy at seven o'clock that the dogs and I waited just inside the door to make our morning rounds.

As I passed the open garage I heard his cry, a series of short, high signals. Then I saw him. He came toward me through the rain, walking on left front leg and right hind leg, using a wounded right front leg as a crutch to keep him upright. His left hind leg was dangling an inch above the ground, and he was almost unrecognizable. He was soaked, of course, but he had also shrunk. Only his great head was its normal size. The rest of him was a narrow slice of bone and fur. I carried him to the house, wrapped him in a towel and for minutes held him tight against my chest to warm him. And through the towel I felt him purr. Carefully then I unwrapped him to examine his wounds. His right front leg was swollen with infection from a gash above his paw. His left hind leg was no longer a leg at all, the bones so pulverized that it hung from the socket like a crooked tassle.

It was not yet eight o'clock, too early to call for help, but I called anyway. "Give me a chance to dress," the young veterinarian said, "then bring him over." My regular vet had sold his practice and moved to an easier life. I didn't know the man who had replaced him, but the time had come. While we waited I placed the watch cat on the kitchen counter, opened a can of tuna and poured a bowl of milk, then held him upright while he ate every scrap of fish. He sniffed the milk suspiciously. He had never tasted cow's milk, but a drop on his nose convinced him that there were things even he had not discovered. He drank it all.

I carried him to the car, another new adventure for a wild cat, and drove the mile through sheeting rain to the animal hospital. There I passed him wrapped in the towel into the doctor's arms. He would be tranquilized, then X-rayed. "The infection indicates this happened some time ago," the vet told me. "But he made it home." The watch cat disappeared into an examining room, leaving me to provide his and my credentials to an assistant who had just arrived. "What's his name?" she asked me.

"He doesn't have a name."

She looked at me, confused. There was a space on the card for Name of Pet. I was a man who had not named his cat. "We'll just put down Black and White Cat," she said.

How could I explain to her the importance of a nameless cat? Why should a name like Blackie or Boots or even Tutankhamun be necessary to confirm our special relationship? Cats are the only friends we have who are still unnumbered, unlisted, unaccounted for. Someone has estimated that America's cat population is twenty million, but he might as well have counted clouds. No one knows or ever will. The watch cat had no need of a name. We both knew who he was. Now, however, he was on record, and because I hadn't named him, was his life less important? These thoughts occurred to me as I stood at the counter in the outer office. "I've known him all his life," I finally said, as if that might matter. "I guess I never needed to call him."

Late that afternoon the veterinarian telephoned. "Your cat was shot," he told me. "The X-rays show the pellets. The rear leg bone is shattered, the front leg badly infected but not broken."

"Can you fix it?" I asked him.

"That's why I called. It will mean a two-to-three-hour operation, a pin to hold the leg together. And it will cost a hundred dollars." He hesitated. "Or I could put him to sleep."

"Will he be able to walk again?"

"Not for several months, but he's young. Young cats heal faster."

"Then fix it," I told him.

I think the young vet was pleased. For him it was a challenge, his reason for practicing. He may not have expected me to invest so much in a nameless country cat, an extra cat when there are already too many. At any rate, he added, "You can take as long as you need to pay me."

The watch cat came home ten days later in a cardboard cat carrier, luggage not for cats who travel but for people who travel with cats. The infection in his front leg had been eliminated. His shattered hind leg had been reassembled, then pinned together with a bolt whose head protruded below the leg joint. My instructions were brief and not quite impossible: confine him for at least the next three months in a room without any surfaces above the floor reachable by a cat. He must not dislocate the leg pin, I was warned. "You'll be surprised how quickly he'll adjust," the veterinarian assured me. I wondered.

I chose the laundry room, furnished only with a washer and dryer and lighted by a high window without a sill. I provided a shallow basket, a cat box and a water bowl, then introduced him to his quarters. Except for the bolted leg he was well again and feeling fit. His coat had recovered its gloss, his tail whipped back and forth and his penetrating stare was more than I could meet. Only his injured leg spoiled the full effect of his royal displeasure. It had been shaved to the hip, sewn in several places, and as he faced me, he looked like an angry monarch with one trouser leg missing.

The weeks of recovery began. I set a routine of frequent visits to present breakfast and dinner, to deal with the cat box and to release him for a half hour each evening to sit on my lap. He enjoyed being held and purred to prove it, arching his back beneath my hand, touching my nose with his. He seemed quite willing to become a pet during these brief moments of escape from confinement. As I carried him back to his cell, however, he struck out at me, catching me with tooth or claw whenever he was faster than I was, an effective, if not recognized form of interspecific communication. As I closed the door I felt the fury in his eyes and heard his silent question: Why?

The void of misunderstanding between men is vast enough. Between men and cats it is infinite. In his famous Cat Bill Veto Adlai Stevenson, as Governor of Illinois, faced the impossibility of legislating cat behavior. "The problem of cat versus bird," he wrote, "is as old as time. If we attempt to resolve it by legislation, who knows but what we may be called upon to take sides as well in the age-old problems of cat versus dog, bird versus bird, and even bird versus worm." Why, then, do men shoot cats? Because, I suppose, they are there.

I brought the watch cat a present. A friend of mine invited me to spend a morning on his small boat exploring the spring perimeters of our replenished reservoir. He could fish; I would go along for the ride. It was a perfect day for me, although not quite perfect for him. In three hours he caught only one small trout, and, self-proclaimed provider that he was, he decided to tell his wife he hadn't fished at all. He gave me the trout. I carried the fish home and laid it before the watch cat as proudly as a mighty hunter returns with a meal for his family. He sniffed it, then limped to his basket. I had to clean the trout, filet and broil it before he would taste it. "You'll be surprised how quickly he'll adjust," the veterinarian had promised. I was.

In early May I carried the watch cat back to have the leg pin removed. Bone and cartilege had formed sufficiently to allow unassisted nature to complete the reconstruction. Even then, however, he was not allowed to leave his plaster and porcelain cell. His leg, now slightly splayed, needed more time to heal, but by the first week in July it was strong enough to carry him from room to room, then from house to yard, finally to the fields he loves.

Off he trotted in three-quarter time, searching out his old paths, checking his lookout points, pushing his posted territory outward. Nor is he earthbound. Once again I meet his eyes at sunrise above the roof edge, along the ladder limb, at the fence top where again he performs as scout for his relatives. Later, he may walk with us along our path, but not for long. With a backward flash of unblinking eyes he leaves us, tail high, to go his velvet way.

Our world is so well explored, so well explained that we hunger for strangeness, wanting to believe that Bigfoot exists, that there is life on other stars. But look again. Perhaps there is a parallel reality just above your head, a watch cat with a crooked leg and angry, golden eyes. If so, don't shoot. He means no harm.

The Last Roundup

I have just completed my last roundup. I have decided I will never make a cattleman, selling my herd at the weekly auction when the price of beef is up, the young cattle fat on summer pasture, and before early frost makes the purchase of alfalfa necessary. That cattle should be sold in the prime of life is an accepted fact of country life, accepted, that is, by all but me, but something must be done. Beef cattle are not raised to grow old, nor is there room in my small pasture for a next generation. The alternative I chose this year proved to be as traumatic as sending my heifers off to the auction block, and it convinced me to get out of the cattle business. My daughter Jeremy and I long ago gave up naming our spring calves — Sergeant Pepper, Corporal Salt, Lieutenant What's-his-name — but even nameless calves have by September become part of the family. Once again the calves delivered in March, auction numbers still pasted high on their hips, the ordeal of cattle prod, shouting auctioneer, slamming gates and laughing cowboys still fresh and terrifying, have come to trust us. They allow Jeremy to scratch their backs. They follow me while I move irrigation pipes, nudging me along with a bloat block in my arms, watching me with soft, dark eyes under mascaraed lashes. By now I have become friend and provider, dependable and presumably vegetarian.

My way of avoiding the awful day when I must betray their trust, hiding out in the house while they are loaded and carried off to the sales yard, was to find a man with a bull and a dream of a larger herd. With this alternative in mind, I bought heifers this year, intending to keep them until they were ready for home and husband, then send them off as happy brides. This alternative solution has sustained us for six months.

At the end of September I placed an ad in the local paper: For Sale! Six Year-old Heifers for Breeding Only. I suppose I was overly optimistic. My six young heifers were a mixed bag, neither purebred nor the proper cross between Angus and Hereford known as white face and locally favored for their beef. They were fat and frisky, however, and ready for a bull. That's about all they had to offer. No one called the first week, and as the ad ran out I had to admit my chances of finding a buyer who would agree to my terms were small. Cattle were plentiful, pasture was running out, and no cattleman with any economic sense would agree to my terms, which were to promise in return for a lower price not to sell the heifers for slaughter. I ran the ad a second week, growing more nervous as September turned into fall and the six heifers appeared at the corral gate each morning expecting breakfast, their morning moos echoing in their sinuses. It was all I could do to face them.

And then I found a buyer. He called from a town twenty miles away, making him already a foreigner and accordingly strange. He had just bought twenty acres of raw land, he told me, had put in an irrigation system and was now ready to decorate his pasture with cattle. He assured me before I asked that he could never sell a cow for slaughter. He wanted a family and had already made arrangements to rent a bull. He sounded more than strange. He sounded crazy. He drove right over to meet my heifers, bringing a six-pack of beer to share with me and a pocket filled with apples for the girls, as he was already calling them. We toasted the sale, and before he left he told me he had already named the smallest heifer Molly. He would send a cattle trailer and two men to move the herd. He could hardly wait. I had found the only man in all this cattle country less qualified than I to own a cow.

I don't approach a roundup like The Virginian, downing a big breakfast at sunup, assigning cowboys to point and drag, shouting "Head 'em up, move 'em out" to grizzled hands. Instead, I told my innocent buyer to move his trailer into the corral the night before, to fill it with choice alfalfa and to allow the heifers time to investigate the vehicle at leisure. All night long I heard them climbing in and out, their hooves banging against the metal floor, and by the morning of the roundup they were waiting beside the trailer for more alfalfa. The strange vehicle had become a breakfast room in the middle of the corral, and I was able to close the gate leading to the pasture without arousing their suspicions. If it had not been our last morning together it would have seemed like a quiet family gathering, horses looking on from outside the fence, dogs wagging, everywhere damp noses turned toward me. Breakfast would not be served on time, but I distributed carrots and scratched a back or two. "Don't worry," I kept telling them, but only I was nervous.

It was after ten when my buyer arrived with two young cowboys brandishing circus whips, their hats pulled low across their foreheads to indicate determination. As they approached the corral, the heifers bunched in a corner. They had memories of men in western hats and were taking no chances. "I'd better go in first," I told them and walked toward the cattle. The tamest of the group, whose new name was Molly, recognized me and came forward. I reached out a hand and pulled a few burrs from her forelock. You can't allow a bride to go off to her bull with burrs in her forelock. The rest moved closer, feeling more secure now that I had joined them.

I carried an armful of alfalfa into the trailer while the heifers gathered around, still uncertain about the two cowboys looking on. Just as I backed out to allow them to step into the breakfast room, one of the young Clint Eastwoods entered the corral. "We'll load 'em," he called. He couldn't allow a bunch of beef to do what they were supposed to do without whips and whoops. His partner followed, moving in behind the cattle. That ended the morning roundup. The heifers backed off, then scattered to the four corners of the corral while the two cowboys snapped their whips and ran after them. As the dust rose around us, the buyer and I stood outside the fence, each of us horrified to watch our transaction turn into a wild rodeo. The six heifers by now were desperate. They charged along the fence lines, heads lowered, forcing the cowboys to climb to the rails to avoid being trampled.

The cattle bunched then in a corner, breathing heavily and glaring red-eyed at me. The cowboys once again moved in, whips twitching, sweat streaking their faces. "Got 'em now," one called to us, as if he had planned the whole maneuvre and was intending to carry the cattle to the trailer. He took a step toward the angry heifers. That was the last step. They plunged against the cedar-rail fence which gave way under nearly four-thousand pounds of pressure, and ran off into the pasture, heels flying, tassle tails streaming.

I felt sorry for my buyer. He had come with beer and apples, with dreams of heifers grazing in his new pasture. His dream would not come true that day or even the next. He stayed while his hired hands repaired my fence, then apologized to me and the cattle for such unmannerly behavior. He seemed to cheer up slightly when I promised delivery within the week, provided that he kept his cowboys away from my cows.

The cattle trailer remained in the center of the corral, and every morning I left alfalfa inside it. At first, the heifers came down after dark to climb inside for a late but quiet breakfast, but within two days the roundup was forgotten and once again I was a friend. By the third morning they followed me into the trailer, blocking my escape so that I stood pinned against the wall while they ate. But cows are not smart. If they were, the western frontier would still begin at the Hudson River. There is in most cattle trailers an escape hatch large enough for a man to squeeze through, and that morning while their jaws revolved I ducked out of the trailer, walked around it and quickly shut the tailgate. It was deceitful, I admit, but in the continuing contest between man and cow, the man's only effective weapon is quiet guile.

My buyer was delighted. He hurried over with another six-pack, insisting that we toast my success while the girls finished breakfast. Then he hitched his pickup to the trailer and headed home. I followed to see the heifers settled, and as I left him he was chasing them across the pasture with an apple in his hand.

P.S.

I received a call on Christmas morning. "You're going to be a grandfather," an unfamiliar voice announced. My two daughters were in the kitchen preparing our Christmas dinner, neither of them married or careless. "Gee," I answered without enthusiasm. "Molly's pregnant," the voice cried.

Then I placed the caller. "Congratulations to you both," I told him.

"Oh, I've been congratulating her," he told me, "and we're having a party. You've got to be here."

"I'll try," I promised, but I knew I wouldn't make it. An ex-cattleman at a calf shower could lose his image.

My Son, The Colt

What a week it has been. My colt has gone off to college. He walked all the way, his contribution to clean air, and looked quite scholarly walking along the roadside, eyes on the path, mind on his education. Still, I can't quite believe it. It seems like only yesterday that he was gelded.

I remember my dilemma a year and a half ago when Mattei was a thriving yearling and the choice between raising a stallion or a gelding was still mine. My veterinarian believed that to geld was best, and I accepted his advice and invited him over for the ceremony. When he arrived, I asked him to remove his western hat because my horses hate cowboys, and I didn't want him to make the wrong impression. Then I accompanied him into the corral to meet my colt.

Administering anesthesia to a large colt takes three people. While I held the lead rope and my daughter Jeremy clutched a bottle filled with watery liquid, Dr. John guided a long rubber tube to a needle in Mattei's neck. At this moment I changed my mind about gelding, but it was too late. My colt was already groggy, I was holding the rope, and retreat was impossible.

Mattei sank softly to the ground where I was assured by his doctor he would sleep in peace. Dr. John moved off to prepare for surgery, my daughter slipped out of sight, and I stood by.

As the surgeon returned, his knife in his hand, Mattei awoke, and in the wild tangle of hooves and rope I found myself flat on my back in the corral, dust swirling around me and the good doctor hovering over me.

"Wait, it's me," I cried.

The vet backed off, blinking dust from his eyes while I struggled to my feet. "That was a close one," Dr. John said, laughing his kindly laugh.

I saw Mattei then, lying peacefully beside me, sound asleep. A few moments later he was on his feet again, aparently feeling no discomfort, but wobbling badly to starboard. Dr. John and I stood on either side of him, propping him up until his head cleared. Then, off Mattei walked to his mother.

"You made the right choice," my veterinarian assured me.

"So did you," I told him warmly.

"Under precisely controlled conditions," biologist George Wald has written, "an animal does as he damn pleases." My colt has devoted the past year to proving Wald's theory. He has outwitted all who have tried to substitute human sense for horse sense, leaving a corral full of broken ropes and broken men. He has submitted willingly to long hours of rubbing and scratching, only to move quickly out of range at the sight of a saddle or a whiff of a stranger. His education has been for him perfectly adequate. He can spot a carrot in my pocket a field away, gallop for joy on a frosty morning, nuzzle his mother out of the way at the hay crib. The sound of the lawnmower is his signal for fresh-cut grass in summer, and the sun on his back at noon reminds him that a nap is a country privilege all of us enjoy. All this he has learned in his short life. What more for him is necessary?

But a young horse who has not felt the cinch or chewed a bit or carried the weight of a girl on his back is not an educated horse. And so Mattei has gone off to college. His tuition is not much less than my oldest daughter's college fees, and he has other things in common with Nicole. Both are vegetarians and neither writes to me. Presumably, both will be better equipped to survive in a complex society.

As Mattei and I passed Dr. John's driveway on our walk to college, I heard a soft snort and felt the pull of the lead rope. For a moment he stopped and turned to glare in the direction of the veterinarian's house. Then we continued. Rememberance of things past was brief and not worth thinking about on such an exciting day.

A Walk into Spring

There is always a day in March when, patience exhausted, I go in search of spring. I take a walk around my yard. It is my first circuit of the territory since the last October mowing, and it happens while spring is still the sum of very small parts. March is the time, and walking the way to see each minor miracle.

On my first day as the owner of a small portion of California country I discovered the value of walking. I stood at my fenceline and looked across at my neighbor's pasture, six times the size of mine; I looked beyond to the hills of a ranch a thousand times the size of his; finally, I saw the faraway horizons of a national forest. At that moment my own piece of this country seemed insignificant. But then I began to walk from one end of my pasture to the other, seeing for the first time wild flowers almost too small to be noticed, winding trails hidden at weasel-eye level, and I felt much better. Now when my neighbor rides his fencelines I walk mine, and the time it takes to make our separate circuits is the same. By walking slowly I have come to realize how large my small world is, and I have seen it all.

I never take this first March walk alone. Ahead of me and already half way around the house my two small dogs run fast. When they stand still, long hair covers their eyes. If they are to help me find whatever it is I search for they must run so that the wind blows their bangs and they can see what I see.

Also, my flock of bluejays follows at varying distances. They know that if I discover spring I will do the digging for them, and they are noisy with hope that this will be the day. And then my old cat, who lives on the roof when the sun is warm, follows our path with a circle of her own around the eaves. There may be others following us, but these are the regular members of our spring safari.

My house sits at the center of a wreath of pines, fruit trees and junipers. At ground level the lawn circles the house, passing islands of birches still bundles of white sticks in March. The grass bubbles up in places where the heat of spring collects, while in others it lies matted and old under the dead weight of continuing frosts. On the north side of the house the lawn narrows into a path of continual shade between high walls of fruit trees selected for their blossoms, not their fruit, and clumps of bottlebrush. Once I took my daughter Susie's hand to lead her on this circuit of the yard. She admired politely until we reached this small enclosed area. "It's like a park," she cried as we walked between green walls. I realized then that because her vision was so limited this was the only part of the yard she could see completely, that to appreciate any segment of our surroundings we must see it all and that it didn't matter how small it was, only that it was complete to our eyes. I walk through this shaded corridor now seeing it as she did, aware of its miniature beauty. I still call it Susie's Park.

The lawn widens to the west where the suns of all seasons warm its roots and where my lawn gopher works his way from one explosion to the next. Here the signs of spring are everywhere. Partially hidden, the first daring dandelion blooms below frost tips. At the edge of the grass the reincarnation of a snapdragon lives again. A plumless plum seasons the grass with pink petals, while on my side of the pasture fence the first field flowers, a species of wild radish, purple in safety, out from under the hooves of the horses. The lawn stream spreads to the southeast, the circling cedars and junipers crowding its banks, always holding the circle we live within. Beyond the trees the larger circumference of pasture where heavy rains have created pillows of burr clover, puffing up the pasture floor before the soil is warm enough for grass. Beyond, another circle of early spring we hardly know.

But our first walk into spring is the walk around my yard, and it always takes longer than it should to reach my door again. Like my daughter, I have looked ahead only a little way, but, like her, I have seen it all.

Mourning Becomes A Dove

Once again we come to the time of year known to some in these parts as Dove Season. It is a season both for and against a bird called the Western Mourning Dove. In its favor, because it is a seed eater, the Mourning Dove thrives in August. In its disfavor, because it is considered by the state to be a game bird, the dove faces a world bristling with dove hunters. On the theory that it is always best to know your adversary, especially if you are new to the game of birds, I have gone to the experts for some facts about the Mourning Dove.

I called upon Margaret Millar, whose book *The Birds And The Beasts Were There* has been my companion since its publication, because Mrs. Millar sees birds in all their varieties where most of us see merely a path through the trees. From her I borrowed Dawson's *The Birds of California* to read about the Mourning Dove.

The Mourning Dove, then, is a robin-size bird with an ancestry older than ours and relatives throughout the world. The passage from *The Song of Solomon* celebrating spring, "The voice of the turtle is heard in the land," refers to this same bird, who is also known as a turtle dove and a wild dove. No one, it seems, has done well with its various names, it being in no way turtle-like, its song not mournful but an expression of lively desire, and its nature gentle, not wild. But, of course, nature's creatures have had nothing to do with naming themselves. No bear would choose to be called Grizzly; no sandpiper would want to be called Least; nobody, for that matter, would go out of his way to be called Irving. (But there is a noble bird called the Townsend Solitaire.)

The Mourning Dove, seen only as a blur among friends, is a drab specimen, but actually its wings are edged in bluish gray, its throat is white, its bill black, its eyes shadowed with pale blue, and there is a patch of royal purple on the upper side of its neck. Also, Dawson points out that its feet are "lake red." All in all, a colorful bird. The average weight of the dove is three-and-one-half ounces with males somewhat larger, females somewhat smaller, and because usually only the pectoral muscles are considered edible, this year's limit of ten birds equals the meat in one hamburger.

The sound of the Mourning Dove is spelled out as "Wheeew Hewh heeeooo," which is probably why doves don't bother with spelling. (People who try to spell bird calls are the subject of a study not being undertaken in these pages, but they are every bit as baffling as any bird.) To this call is added a whistling wind note caused by the flapping of the dove's wings. By all acounts, the Mourning Dove is a great lover and a poor housekeeper, its nest a disgraceful bundle of sticks thrown together on the fly, so to speak, and using any convenient tree stump, fence post, or the ground itself. The female lays a couple of white eggs in this slovenly pad several times a year, and when her young are large she straddles the whole pile like the last tackler in a small boys' football game. Still, she is gentle, loving and desirable. You can't have everything.

The Mourning Dove's capacity for seeds is amazing. Sixty-four hundred foxtail seeds were found in a dove's stomach, the contents of a single meal, and the dove requires several such meals a day. It has been estimated that a dove consumes the equivalent of ten acres of potential weeds each year and is credited with having been a major factor in the economic development of California. It seems paradoxical that a farmer who kills his quota of doves each season also spends large sums to rid his pasture of weeds.

There is some difficulty in telling the difference between a pigeon and a dove. Dawson clarifies the confusion, or contributes to it, by stating that a pigeon is gullible, stupid and larger. I hope that helps.

Ounce for ounce, the meat on a Mourning Dove equals the meat on a fat sardine, but there are other virtues in a sardine which seem to tip the scales in in its favor as an appetizer. For one thing, the sardine comes in a can. A friend of mine finds sardines useful in maintaining a proper respect for him by his tropical fish. When they seem to forget who's boss, he sits down in front of his aquarium and eats sardines.

Once again it is dove season. There are those, it seems, who can hardly wait.

At The Death of An Oak

At exactly 2:05 on a recent October Friday morning I heard a tree die. I did not know then that that was what I heard. I was awakened by a wrenching burst of noise, as if a large animal had torn out a section of a fence. The sound was particularly shattering because there were no other night sounds to absorb it's edges, and the night itself, like most country nights, in early fall, was soft as cotton. Fog fingers had crept through mountain passes to lie low across the valley, and the world was wrapped in owls' wings.

My dogs and I are occasionally disturbed in those silent hours by the strident meeting of cats, an eruption of pure hatred chilling us with its reminder that even our small world is never long at peace. We have also heard death before and have huddled closer, horrified at the time it takes a small animal to die. Death and night are partners.

The sound we heard that Friday morning was not a mortal sound. There was destruction in it, and it was heavy with blunder. It set the dogs off on wild cascades of barking, interrupted by baffled silences and dashing from door to door. There were also fear and the urge to hide, but for me these were accompanied by the uncomfortable knowledge that I was the only one to face a night crisis that would not be put off. I waited, listening for the scrape of hooves on tarmac, shrinking from the thought of a night roundup of horses. But there was no aftersound. Outside the silence had returned, deeper now like the silences that follow final endings. Inside, the dogs continued to puzzle, not quite convinced that they had dreamed the sound. They had not, and neither had I, so I wrapped myself up for a search, found a flashlight and walked to the corral gate. The flashlight beam picked out the horses' heads. All accounted for. No broken gates, no sagging fence posts. I returned to bed wondering how such a crash could leave no trace.

Under the iron lid of early morning I searched again and found no change in my fencelines, no apparent change in my skyline. Not until the sun broke through did I see the tree. After that I could see nothing else. It lay just beyond my pasture in a flower field, and it seemed so much larger than any tree I'd ever seen before. It was a live oak, it's branches still alive with clusters of dark green leaves, but now the branches lay strewn across the ground. The huge trunk that had for so long supported them had broken in two. The old oak had simply laid down on a windless October night and died.

We look upon death in this country every day, but the ends of shorter lives are common, and we pass by without a backward glance. Even the death of trees by axe or lightning shaft is nothing remarkable in our wooded world. But the death of this tree was something else. Born with a vanished race of men, destined to live a century or two, this tree had seemed immortal. An oak that has sheltered Chumash hunter and pioneer does not die in a moment of my lifetime without a struggle, without a push.

The great tree lies there now unattended and unmourned, as out of place on its side as a beached whale. I have gone each morning to sit by the fence, still shaken by the sight of it. It could have fallen to the south instead of the east, crushing my fence beneath it, but even a falling tree means no harm, and this one did none.

Its time was on some calender of eons before the imagining of men. It parted from its roots no longer able to sustain it and lay down in a flowered field. What final effort proved too much I could not tell. Perhaps, one termite bite too many or the weight of one last bird.

An oak's only journey is this last fall from the sky. This one fell for me to hear, and I shall remember it. Somehow it seems appropriate that it fell on a pillow of marigolds.

The Visitor

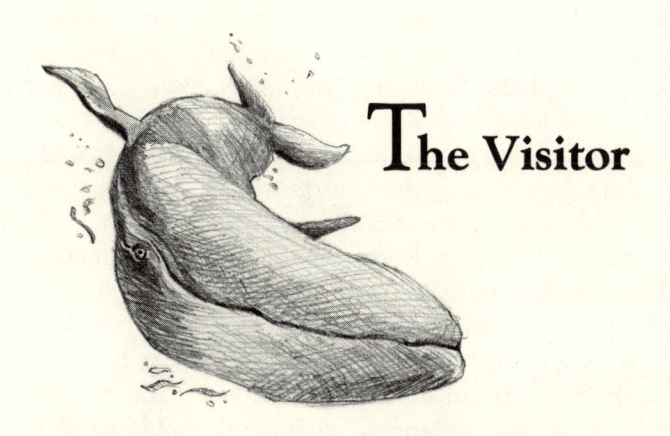

Recently, I became a whale watcher for a day by joining a Sierra Club-sponsored cruise to the waters around Anacapa Island off the coast of southern California to search for a glimpse of the gray whale on his annual trip from the Bering Sea to Mexican waters where these whales conceive and give birth. It was a sunless January morning with light rain mixing with sea spray on our faces, a morning grim for whale watchers, hardly worth noticing for whales. As the small power boat filled with the curious sped across our bow toward a rolling back, while we passengers in the larger craft rushed from side to side to point, to stare, to feel anew the distance between us and a whale, a pod of grays continued on course, breaking the sea's surface, then diving to reappear hundreds of yards away. Once that morning we happened to be close enough to a traveling foursome to see the barnacles clinging like buttons to their flanks. "They must itch," a well muffled woman beside me observed, seeking, as we all were, some small sense of communion.

Well, they do. And there are a few other sensations we share with whales, but too few to give us the warm sense of understanding we seek between ourselves and this embattled beast. Whales are social, talkative, and compassionate. They are thin skinned and feel the bite of barnacles, get sick from the wrong food, and have their moments of fun. Some wear whiskers; some are bullies. Some bump their heads on rocks, and now and then one gets confused and heads for shore.

Most of what is known about whales emphasizes how really little is known, deepening the mystery of the whale, tantalizing those who try to understand him. The songs whales sing, for instance, have been described by human listeners as sounding like the malfunctions of plumbing, as incomprehensible to us as the short-wave chatter of sailors must be to whales. Yet, their singing sends messages of joy, of warning, of discovery to other whales. The voyage of the gray whale, a nine-thousand-mile circle six months in duration, is a baffling performance to us: instinctive, we decide, but among communicating minds millions of years experienced who is to separate instinct from directed learning? The spectacle of whales copulating in midair above Scammon's Lagoon jolts our assumptions again, perhaps because we've never tried it.

Nor can we imagine what it can be like to live half a century or more without ever touching bottom, without sitting down or drying off or curling up. We have never seen a whale die of natural causes, nor can we know the routine of their lives. Most incredible of all, we will never know why the whale, once his progenitors had made their way out of the primordial slime to become air-breathing land creatures, chose to return to the sea. The wasted eons necessary to grow legs and lungs, to develop a sense of smell, to enjoy a sun warmed rock, it seems, were casually tossed away as the whale settled for flukes and flippers and holes in the top of his head. To man on the beach, to us aboard the converted Coast Guard cutter *Paisano* huddled leeward of the biting spray, whales must either be crazy or they must know something we missed along the way. Either possibility rattles our thwarted curiosity.

Certainly the discovery a thousand years ago that whales could be caught and killed, that whale parts were useful and therefore valuable have helped us to live with the mystery of the whale. The number of men since Aristotle who have tried to figure him out is fewer than the number of whalers active in a single year of modern whaling. We have proved, at least, that if brainweight were a measure of the mind, whales would have been calling the offshore shots over the entire span of human existence, although it is doubtful that whales would have invented the harpoon. They prefer krill.

Whale lore compensates for its inadequacy with poundage. Whale size makes all statistics awesome, but while a whale heart can be weighed, its intestines measured, we know little of its temperature controls, its mechanism for pressure adjustments, how far it can see, or why, having shed legs and arms, it still retains an apparently useless nose.

On a Saturday morning in late January, the second month in the gray whale's annual winter vacation, forty chilled and silent passengers boarded the *Paisano*, now in service as a student-tour boat, to the islands off the Santa Barbara channel. Before our departure a Sierra Club host gathered us all on the forward deck where he attempted to read his name and his greeting from a paper flapping in his mittened hands. "Just call me Dobie," he concluded, unable to read what had been written, "and ask me any questions you like."

But as we headed for Anacapa, the sky refusing to respond to the rising sun, the sea black and green and forbidding, Dobie confessed to me that this was only his second whale watch and that all he knew about gray whales was contained on a single mimeographed page he handed out: Rhachianectes glaucus, color grayish black, size 35 to 45 feet, weight 24 to 37 tons. "My wife usually takes out parties," he explained, "but she's sick today. She knows a lot more."

Southeast of Anacapa, which rises from the sea like the hump of a greater whale, its shoreline a thin rim of rocks and occasional patches of black sand, we saw our first whales. There were three, rolling on the waves, then, with a flip of their flukes, diving before our captain could reach them. Four times we pursued whale pods leeward of the island before we happened to be close enough to see the barnacles, but to stand within a dozen feet of a moving whale carrying his parasites along to tropic inlet is to feel a greater sense of the void which separates us from them. We leaned against the port rail looking down at the largest creature alive and shivered in our padded jackets.

Then the whales were gone. The parade had passed us, to be reviewed tomorrow by watchers farther south, a month of swimming still ahead before the moment that made it all worthwhile. "Not many this year," Dobie told us. "They're spooked. Maybe earthquakes." We cruised the perimeter of the island under the curious eyes of sea lions resting in rock cradles, pelicans ruffling in the wind. We anchored in a small harbor and were taken ashore to eat our picnic lunches, cold food on wet black sand under the primitive eaves of the crust of Anacapa, an island said to be older than its neighboring continent, useless to man and animal. Above us its shell had been pierced here and there, spilling volcanic debris into the sea. There was no sun, no shelter, and we waited impatiently to leave.

Back aboard the *Paisano* we were offered the choice of continuing our cruise for what was left of the afternoon or of returning to the marina. Unanimously we elected to go home, the possibility of sighting more whales no longer tempting. "I'm glad I'm not a whale," the muffled lady beside me said. "At least, we have a choice."

Heading for the harbor and home it seemed to me that of all the insuperable differences that divide men and whales, that separate whales from all else that lives, it is not the element in which they must remain, nor their size, nor their struggle to survive as mammals in a coldblooded world. Only the whale on the changing surface of the sea is homeless and without a nest. Every creature is sustained by protecting walls of shell or cave or crevice. The houses men and insects build, the overhanging limbs that shelter the grazers, the coves and tunnels and indentations of the earth provide physical and psychological retreat for every living creature except the whale. Called the king of the sea, master of his environment, the whale, in fact, is neither. Because nature, often supremely inconsistent, denied the whale the one ability that could save him, to be able to breathe under water, the smallest fish statistically has a better chance for survival.

Docked and once again connected with the land, we whale watchers hurried away from the sea, some taking the shortest route to the sustenance of the marina bar, others climbing into cars to drive home, all of us again within our chosen walls. Only the gray whales continued their unending voyage.

The gray whale swims between two worlds, underequipped for either, a stranger to both. Exiled by nature, doomed by man, he is a creature frightening to us not because of his harmless bulk, but because if he were not real he would be unimaginable. He is the world's last nomad, forbidden the comforting depths of the sea, the havens of the shore. He is a visitor who can never go home.

April Eyes are Wider Eyes

To me April is all eyes. Perhaps, this is because there is so much to see, or maybe it's because April eyes are beautiful. Wherever I have gone this month April eyes are on me, all about me, wide and clear and larger than eyes usually are. It is possible to see farther in April, for the weight of summer days has not yet settled between me and the horizon, nor has the residue of afternoon lingered into morning. April is washed early and dries slowly.

Or, perhaps, I notice April eyes because I have become more conscious of what it is to be sightless than the sighted usually are. I have lived with blindness and have watched the mind adjust to it, the other senses heightened and moving in to fill the void. Not to see in April is the cruelest fate of all, but to feel April, to touch her softness, to gather her into yourself, to know her vaulted dome is there, are gifts bestowed especially upon the blind, and April also to them is wide eyed, bushy tailed and marvelous.

On this April morning I thought of what it would be like to awaken without seeing, as my daughter so often did, and wondered how she would know it was April instead of March or October. What is there about April that is unique, even to the blind? I arose in self-created darkness to find out.

I have a clock that strikes the hour. I believe in hearing as well as seeing time, in spite of modern clock technology which first eliminated the strike, then the tock and finally now even the face of time. My old clock was striking six while I waited for April signs. They came. The first indications of sunrise I heard in my animals. A dog yawned with an extra squeak of delight he only makes on special mornings. Another got up to scratch. Finally, cat's feet began their slow walking in place on my chest as claws were sharpened for another day. It was morning.

I can walk through the rooms of my house in total darkness without bumping into anything. This is partly because I know it so well. It is also because I have so little furniture that, if he knew the pattern of the rooms, a stranger could also walk blindly through them. I dressed and walked with eyes closed to the wide glass door leading to the backyard, dogs around me, cat tail curling at my knees. I pulled the door open and walked out to the edge of the grass. I stopped there. I had already gone far enough to know it was April. The trees at the fringe of the lawn crackled with bird conversation. (Birds seem to do most of their talking before breakfast. I would never make a successful bird.) The air was cool, but not frosty, clear, not damp. A horse whinnied somewhere in front of me, so I knew he saw me. And I could smell April in the flowers I had planted. It was the purple smell of spring. I could touch April by reaching out to the hanging pots of blossoms, open all night like some drugstores. With my eyes tightly shut I knew what month it was.

Then I opened my eyes and saw the eyes around me. Brown eyes of waiting dogs, bottomless eyes of horses, their horizontal pupils dark blue, yellow eyes of my cat watching me from the roof edge. Later, we drove to the library to read what others had thought about April eyes. On the way we met a young girl out for a walk, blue eyes matching the fiesta floweers along her path. I might have known it. I'd been scooped by Shakespeare: "The April's in her eyes"; by Longfellow: "Within her tender eye the heaven of April with its changing light"; and George Dillon had written, "Of slender girls with suddenly wider eyes."

I thought again about what it must be to be sightless in April and knew for a fact that it is not possible. My daughter must have seen April every year, as I had this morning, in her mind's eye.

We Can't All Be Cats

This is a cat column, provoked by the latest cat rumor, edged by the sick humor of a cat hater, inspired by a gray velvet cat with lime eyes and a built-in smile. Her name is Liki. She has a kidney problem.

My cat has been more on my mind lately, I think, because we are meeting more often at odd cat hours. All animals follow a routine of their or our choosing and are happier when it is consistent. Cat routines, like cats themselves, are less predictable because cats do not follow us, but walk a parallel path. Surprise is not only their weapon but their privilege. For my cat to come home at sunset to the dinner she knows is waiting is routine. For her to spend a part of the night on my bed is also normal. Even a noon appearance in the patch of sunlight on the patio, there to lie on her back long enough to warm her considerable girth, is only to be expected.

Lately, however, the cat in my family has come home more often and stayed longer, sometimes not getting out of bed until late afternoon, often disposing of her nightly gopher early enough to settle in with us before midnight. She and I have been meeting in places we never go together, in the hayloft, in the pasture, on an eye-level branch.

Now and then her old ailment flares up, and she wilts until a cup of alfalfa tea is trickled down her throat through an eye dropper. The tea works like a plumber's helper, restoring her system, enabling her to resume her normal adjacency to the rest of us. We all feel much better when Liki is again on patrol or chirping for dinner or smoothing her whiskers against the nearest cheek.

To live with a cat is to understand man's age-old admiration for an animal he has never understood. It is to recognize in cats what we have lost in ourselves as our dependence increases and we follow a track we did not lay. A cat is still without a number on file at city hall. A cat prefers to cross our road, not follow it. A cat on welfare is unthinkable. We may prefer the company of dogs, but we like to believe we were once, and may again be, like cats.

Which brings me to the rumor. It has been supposed by some wishful anthropologist that we are descended, not from apes, but from cats. Can that be? We are at last beginning to accept a long and painful transition from fur to skin, from branch to cave, from fang to club as our brain weight increased and language permitted sociability. We see in the ape a caricature of ourselves and laugh uneasily when he behaves too much like us. But can we be descended from cats?

The more I observe my cat the more I doubt it. I lack her patience at a closed door, her satisfaction with solitude, her timing. I lack her alliance with the night and her freedom from worry, her ability to express delight without opening her mouth, her silent approach. Besides, my thumbs are all wrong.

As long as there are cats we will have something to admire, something science cannot explain, something we can kill but never conquer, something we meet but never own. Cats remind us of our clumsiness, our misplaced pride, our questionable lovableness. It is not surprising that our vanity prods us toward proof that we were once catlike. How a cat would smile at that!

About that cat hater. It seems that after he swings his cat by the tail they spit at each other, and . . .

But there is no space for more of him. There never was.

How to Spend
A Two-Dog Night

Almost everybody who listens to music younger than Lawrence Welk's is aware that Three Dog Night was the name of a rock group. The number of people, however, who know that a three-dog night is colder than a two-dog night, although not so cold as a four-dog night in that part of Russia inhabited by people called Samoyeds may be somewhat smaller. The few who manage to get any sleep on even a two-dog night may be counted on the toes of one Samoyed. In the interests of those other than Samoyeds who seem to be too cold to care one way or the other, I will address myself to the art of sleeping with two dogs. For the few who have already mastered the technique I will later add a cat, although I urge beginners to leave the cat out, at least for the first few nights.

To achieve any sort of success (sleep) certain arbitrary conditions must be assumed, the first one being a king-size bed. There is no point in lying down in anything smaller. While the size and breed of dog is not important, (people who sleep with dogs know that before the night is over everybody collects into a pile), the condition of the dogs may be. Very thin dogs, for instance, are lumpy. (You'll notice that the Samoyeds have developed very comfortable dogs.)

I have selected the two-dog minimum because, as we shall see, it is the only way to stay in bed at all. The key word here is leverage. All dogs spend the night pressed tightly against their human bedfellows, but no two dogs ever sleep on the same side. This is, in part, an expression of the Let Sleeping Dogs Lie principle. It is also to create leverage. Because the human is always in the middle, held tightly in place by dogs and the additional need to be wrapped in a blanket, while dogs prefer to sleep on top of the same blanket, restlessness and recurring cramps are difficult to handle. Here is a tip: When you first lie down and before the dogs settle against each side of you, spread your legs three inches apart, stiffen and hold out no matter how great the pressure. When the time comes to turn over, bring the legs quickly together under the now slightly slackened blanket and revolve quickly before the dogs wake up. As soon as you have assumed a new position, allow for those crucial three inches again. Otherwise, you're a mummy for the rest of the night.

Never spread the legs more than three inches, however. A dog's favorite place to sleep is in the hollow created by legs too widely spread, and once settled he and you are frozen into position until morning. (There is a way out of this trap, but it is difficult to describe without slides.) Dogs who prefer to sleep on their backs must be given turning space three times the height of the dog at the shoulder. Dogs who like pillows may be accommodated if you sleep on your side with the legs scissored so that each dog has an ankle for a chin rest. Above all, beware of curling. When the curl is reversed, both dogs are dislocated, resulting in low growls on both sides of you.

When you are ready to add a cat, position is all important. (This is a trick the Samoyeds have long since mastered.) All cats prefer to sleep in hollows, but no cat will sleep on the same side with a dog. (Remember, you only have two sides.) You must therefore become a triangle. This is accomplished by assuming a horizontal diver's crouch, thereby creating not only three more or less exclusive sides, but two hollows as well. With one dog at you front, the other against your back, the cat can curl into the hollow at the back of you knees, separated from both dogs. All will then sleep soundly.

The Samoyeds have left no written instructions in any language we can decipher for coping with early morning scratching, possibly because they are always awake scratching themselves. They must also have solved the problem of pretending to sleep while being closely scrutinized by various animals, but again they tell us nothing.

Just as well. Too much to remember all at once will keep you awake.

A Continuity of Collies

Shakespeare divided a man's life into seven parts, perhaps, because he never owned a dog. My life, measured by the lives of collies, is better divided by five, each part beginning with a warm-milk breath, needle teeth marks on every handle and the pleasure of watching a great, four-legged puppy learn to balance himself on three. The second of my collie segments was dogless because I was in college and later in the navy, but I made up for that lonesome period by enjoying two at once in the third collie age of my life. From then on my days have been graced by special collies who, like runners in a relay race, have picked up the baton from their predecessors to keep in step with me for a lap or two.

Two months ago the fourth part of my life came to a sad end with the loss of my thirteen-year-old companion. In thirteen years we had come to know each other better than most twosomes by remaining true to ourselves, by being consistent about our habits, by recognizing that friendship changes but does not stiffen with age. Then I lost him. "Old for a collie," I was told, as if a fact of life made any sense. But I know better than those who live one part of their lives with a dog, lose him and vow never to endure the loss again. I found a new collie to accompany me through the fifth part of my life, and, although so far it is an uneven match, we will adjust, he and I. He will learn to stop when he is too far ahead of me to allow me to catch up. I will catch some of his curiosity for a world that is old to me, new to him. For the moment, however, the rest of my animal family joins me in a tighter circle, backsides touching, heads lowered, not quite knowing where to expect the next attack.

If you remember your Pooh stories, you'll recall the morning of Tigger's arrival in the forest, his bouncy approach to all the smaller animals, his meeting with Eeyore. The old donkey walked all around this strange new animal, then asked, "What did you say it was?" Pooh explained that it was a Tigger and that he had just come to join them all. Eeyore thought for a long time and then asked, "When is he going?"

That has been the reaction to Elodio, my new collie puppy. My two small dogs have been stepped on every day. My old fat cat has been circled so often her neck is stiff from keeping an eye on him. And I, heading slowly off to accomplish something at a pace I have developed over long years, the tempo permitted to a man without a deadline for doing things no one else will notice anyway, have been hustled and prodded and circled and challenged.

Tigger kept promising to become quiet and refined as soon as he had found something Tiggers like for breakfast. Elodio makes no false promises. He is, after all, a collie in the best year of his life, and his greatest shock so far has been to discover that all the world is not young. It is his intention, I believe, to change this discrepancy. He is descended from a family of twenty-one champions, but that does not impress either of us. No collie of mine will enter show business. What is important is that he gives me a sense of continuity. He is different from all my other collies because he must be, for in a continuity of collies each must remain distinct and immortally himself. But, like the rest, he is beautiful outside and in, his coat dressed with a royal ruff, his hips covered with sable skirt, his amber eyes soft. And like the rest he has his inconsistencies. He hates to hear me raise my voice, yet he seldom hesitates to raise his own.

I fool myself, I suppose, in thinking that because he is a collie, a breed I know and admire, he somehow connects the dog divisions of my life, that because I again walk beside a collie we are a lifelong pair. But that is the feeling a new collie always gives me, a sense of continuity, the chance to go back and start again.

Homecoming and Going

From the moment I decided to drive across the country to spend a month at the Connecticut farm where my children were born, a place of many beginnings, if not my own, the trip became a going home. I knew, of course, that this could not be true. I had left New England nearly twenty years ago, carrying my family with me, and my return now alone would be a visit, no more. I had been offered the use of a small guest house behind the farmhouse which used to be mine, and I was assured of a warm welcome by neighbors who had known me well. I chose the month of June for my return because I remembered it as a month of dogwood blossoms and early roses, before the mosquitoes and after the mayflies, when city friends would be returning to the country and country friends would not yet be leaving for beach cottages or vacations abroad. This would be my vacation, long overdue, but it seemed to me much more than that.

And with this sense of going home came a disturbing change in my feelings about the small California ranch where I have found such peace and satisfaction, which has been my home for a dozen years in ways that no other in my life has been. Suddenly, it no longer seemed home to me. In those spring weeks before my trip, after winter rains had turned the countryside into deep spring, it never looked more beautiful. Yet, it became someone else's house where I had been a temporary resident, not a place I knew as mine. This was a very disquieting discovery; it almost approached treachery, and it added a rootlessness which, because I would be returning in a month and because it is probably the last house I will ever own, caused me to think of myself late in my life as adrift.

I tried to rationalize these conflicting thoughts of home. I told myself that all of us who move a half dozen times in our lives, whose family generations divide until each member has a different zip code, cannot reverse the process. We burn our bridges, not our mortgages, these days and choose at last to live among our contemporaries, not our relatives. Home is no longer a house we return to where the trees are old and we are always half expected. Still, as I prepared for my trip, I continued to feel that I was not just heading east, but heading home.

This detachment from my present home was made all the more uncomfortable when it came time to leave my family of animals. To them this is home, the only home they know. There was no question of deserting them or dislocating them for my sake, but the thought that I did not belong where they did made our last weeks together uneasy ones for me. And it caused me to make a greater effort to see that none of them would suffer in my absence. My collie would spend the month with my daughter in the city. She is his favorite family member, and I knew that if consulted he would prefer a city vacation with her to a country stay alone. My old cat, on the other hand, must not be moved. Home to her is the roof of the house when the sun is warm, the run of its rooms at night, with meals served at her place on the kitchen counter at her signal. Home to my horses is a spring pasture, an open stable in the heat of afternoons and a forkful of hay for reassurance. My neighbor and her son agreed to stand in for me in these capacities, and even the outside cats would find a meal waiting when the gopher catch was less than filling.

That left my two Lhasas, small dogs whose roots run west to Tibet via Bakersfield and Beverly Hills, whose home has always been wherever I am. They must go with me. Lhasas are fine travelers. Their bangs and large, nearsighted eyes limit sightseeing. They mistake mailboxes for hitchhikers and overturned trash cans for dogs along the road. Their forward tilt gives them the appearance of deep thinkers, and their button noses require several sniffs to absorb a piquant scent, but as traveling companions they are unsurpassed. For one thing, they leave the driving to me. For another, they think I'm almost perfect.

With each family member suitably provided for, I could indulge my fantasy, and I did so in those final days of packing and preparing. Only one upsetting oversight marred that prelude to my departure. Mine is a two-car family of one. I use a Chevrolet pickup for daily driving. For special occasions, trips to the city and evenings when my pants are clean, I drive a Ford Granada with limited space but comfortable seats. This social car is rarely used and is often parked for weeks under a carport, its windows half open to keep it aired. For the cross-country drive I decided to have it serviced, and when I opened the door I found that it had become the home for a mother cat and four new kittens settled in their carpeted nest. My going home caused their eviction, and I apologized, but when his car becomes a kitten factory, I explained to them and to myself, a man has stayed in one place too long.

Although I have flown across America many times and visited most of its large cities, I had never really seen my country. My decision to drive, to avoid cities and wherever possible to take the longer way was also a part of my homecoming. I wanted to meet my country as a man wants to meet his distant relatives, knowing that they will be strangers, but strangers who should be acquainted. Traveling with dogs has been made easier since Americans have mobilized themselves. The interstate highway stops, the franchised motel chains, all accept dogs as inseparable family members. It is no longer even necessary to admit there are dogs in the car when registering, and along the grassy verges of motel parking lots dog owners are pulled past each other as their straining pets revel in the traces of traveling canines. To a dog a room in a Holiday Inn is an intoxicating registry of previous four-legged occupants.

My small dogs quickly settled into the routine of all-day driving, of afternoon check-ins and rooms with a choice of beds. We were together on this great adventure, and they were determined to share it all with me. Together we stood at the south rim of the Grand Canyon as the setting sun gilded its sculptured flanks. We watched an evening thunderstorm roll toward our motel window across New Mexico's strange sedimentary furniture. It was their first thunderstorm, and it established their reactions to the onslaughts that followed. The larger and usually braver dog sat shivering on my lap, her face hidden against me. The smaller, less adventurous struck back at the resounding heavens, but because her strike radius is the crescent beyond her nose, she missed Thor and bit my ankle. Later, we were to drive through hailstones, grasshoppers and between tornadoes, and always each dog behaved this way. They have slept through the vistas of Yellowstone, the overhanging icicles of Glacier Park, the sherbet colors of the Blue Ridge Mountain Parkway, awakening only to the slap of the first pellet on the windshield. For little dogs with short legs and a tendency to sit down from the front they have been around.

Among the highpoints of our days on the road was my return each evening from the motel dining room. With dogs in mind I always ordered beef or chicken and saved enough for them. This sharing prevented my testing local and regional delicacies: walleyed pike in Minnesota, catfish along the Mississippi, and in Fremont, Ohio, Lobster Tails Rutherford B. Hayes, "named after the president that lived in Fremont — a presidential seafood." My return to our room was an occasion only surpassed in Amarillo, where we dined together. The Holiday Inn in that Texas city has installed an energy-saving lock on the air-conditioning system which can be turned on only by inserting the room key. When a guest leaves his room, taking the key with him, air circulation is shut off, creating a lethal vacuum. To save my dogs from suffocation, I ordered our dinners from room service, a Texas steak for me, two Texas hamburgers for them. "No coleslaw, no carrot sticks, no potato chips, no cinnamon apple ring on the hamburgers," I specified, "and no napkins or silverware." Their dinners arrived under plate warmers, the hamburgers nestled in parsley wreathes.

For those with coastal destinations, driving across America in the late twentieth century is similar in some ways to the westward trek of the pioneers. Civilization is left behind, settlements are bypassed, contact with fellow mortals all but eliminated. The routes of the interstate highways have been deviously chosen to avoid distraction, and they are as isolated and endless as wagon trails. No Main Street, no town center, no local traffic slow the interstate traveler whose world for thousands of miles consists of camp grounds, rest areas, highway motels, easy-access coffee shops and service stations. It is a restless, predictable world of homeless nomads, and I wondered as we moved across it about other moving populations, the Bedouins of the Mideast deserts, the wildebeasts of the African plains, America's drifting herds of tourists. What sustains them without a final harbor, never belonging anywhere? After days on the road only the inside of the vehicle remains a place of privacy and personal possessions.

The major motel chains make a well publicized effort to see that each franchised unit resembles every other. This uniformity applies particularly to guest rooms where dimensions, fixtures and furniture are always the same and even the Gideon Bible is open at the same Psalm, the 23rd. After the first two or three days of our trip I was certain that my little dogs believed we were staying in the same room every night, and before a week was out I found it difficult to disagree with them. This motel policy is, of course, successful the world over in making steady customers out of people who never stay in the same place twice. For reasons dangerous to examine, we like to keep moving and to retain the illusion that we are standing still. At the end of each day's travel we entered the room like a returning family, heading for familiar furniture always in the same location, and to compound the deception I even placed the dog's water bowl and dinner bowls in the same place outside the bathroom door, chose the same bed and scattered our belongings in the same sequence. Even the weary faces at the ice machine began to look familiar. Was it possible that if we had continued we would eventually have come to think of that ubiquitous room as our home?

Not all is predictable, nor is every experience quite the same. A motel room in Tulsa, for instance, actually had windows that opened; a service station in Willow, California, employed female attendants who cleaned all the car windows without being asked; a tollgate cashier on the Indiana Turnpike recognized the breed of my dogs. And there are, of course, marked variations in the landscape from state to state. Road signs in New Mexico advertise Indian Jewelry, while those in Missouri push walnut bowls, and across the width of South Dakota a drugstore hawks its wares from every hillside. The empty edges of the interstates also reflect geographic change. In the Texas panhandle the only vertical we saw was a dust devil, while in adjacent Oklahoma suddenly there are trees growing out of bright red soil. Scattered about the undulate fields of the upper Midwest were great wheels of hay, like giant balls of twine about to roll away at the nudge of a prairie dog. In the eastern states the skyline swells into well fed hills, the Smokies, the Ozarks, the Alleghenies, but always the traveler's path is a lonesome trail and he is effectively isolated from the resident. Hungry for a familiar sound, I turned on the car radio each morning, searching for news even of a distant war to confirm my citizenship, but local radio broadcasts are not for us interstate flybyes. They are intended to please the homefolks, attuned to local sentiments and interests, and even tomorrow's weather forecast is meaningless to the listener who tomorrow will be four hundred miles away. In Gallup, an Indian disc jockey played records of tribal drums. In Texas and Idaho and Iowa, the morning news was of cattle auctions and commodity prices. In Oregon, the entertainment was lumber production, in Michigan, fishing rights, in Ohio, labor disputes. We encapsulated strangers are not an audience; we are eavesdroppers.

The aristocrat of the interstates is the trucker, and it is primarily for his convenience and schedule that these fast trucks and pit stops are intended. Rest areas appear at random along the pell-mell path between the oceans, roadside oases which are usually equipped with toilets, picnic grounds, drinking fountains and pet areas. The pet parks we visited were weed patches on the fringes of the rest areas. There, leashed to our dogs, we travelers meet and keep our distance, our common bond, our pets, straining toward greener grass, our common affliction, limbo, thinning our smiles. Meanwhile, the big rigs fill the parking spaces, their drivers asleep on high seats, seemingly as satisfying as family hearths. The rest of us, uncomfortably aware of the adjacent speedway and the miles to go before we sleep, urge our dogs to our cars, fasten our seatbelts and resume speed.

Dog passengers fare better than their chauffeurs in several ways. A waterbowl under the dashboard, a box of crackers behind the front seat, a shady side of the car and the ever-whistling wind make home out of a moving vehicle. They don't know where they're going, but there is no anxiety. Road construction, usually occurring within the last fifty miles of each day's journey, rouses them but never dampens their spirits. Otherwise, the rhythmic slap of paving seams lulls them until I wondered whether mine would be just as happy if we never stopped.

Lhasas, called Lion Dogs of Tibet, are fiercely protective and very loud. Mine awoke at toll booths and gas pumps to bark like maddened mops at every outstretched hand. Toll booths abound between New York and Chicago, and many are staffed with dog lovers anxious to make friends of my two snarling companions. It was safer, I decided, to roll up the window and drive off without my change. Alert at the end of the day, my dogs were still willing to settle beside me for a nap in late afternoons, to sleep again at ten and to return to the road at sunrise. Like me, they love the dawn and seem to share my conviction that the new day will be better than the old.

And then it was. We slowed at the final exit, turned into a two-lane blacktop and headed down a tree tunnel toward our first Connecticut town. We were moving slowly, and bird songs reached us through the open windows of the car. We passed restored old houses whose immaculate lawns reached to the roadside, and each building, older than when last I had seen it, looked newer. Connecticut, the Constitution State, is proud of its history and carefully preserves its past. Here permanence is more permanent than in the west, the houses more deeply rooted, and while they are traded periodically as elsewhere, New England dwellings look more like homes than houses. How good it was to pass familiar corners, to recognize street names and shopping centers. It seemed to me that nothing had changed since I left this venerable country, that it was waiting untouched by two decades more of man's persistence.

My dogs sensed An Arrival and climbed into my lap to get a better view. They were not coming home, I was, but as always they felt my change of heartbeat and adjusted theirs to match. Then we turned into my old street. At first, I hardly knew it. After twenty years the trees had altered outlines, blurred sharp edges, reduced the sky space. I read an unfamiliar name on my mailbox. A boy's bicycle stood in the yard of the farmhouse where only girls had lived. A face appeared at my bedroom window, then withdrew.

We were welcomed, of course, and expected. Our guest house by the river was ready and old friends wanted to be called as soon as we arrived. My little dogs, realizing that this was no overnight stop, ran off to examine trees their predecessors had known, but I continued to feel uneasy there behind the house where I had lived so long ago. Like the face at the window, it seemed preoccupied and only mildly curious. Wherever I looked everything was not quite as I remembered it, but it was not the place that had changed. I had, and when we were greeted by a trio of barking dogs I realized what was wrong. This was a complete community whose tenants were all accounted for. There was no vacancy waiting for us to fill and none would appear when we were gone.

On our way west at the end of June we came one early afternoon to the edge of a summit garden high in the Wyoming Rockies. Within a protecting circle of jagged peaks lay a shallow cradle blanketed with lupin spears and rimmed with drifted snow shrinking in the summer sun. We stood at the roadside looking down into this white and purple bed, filling our lungs with icy fragrant air, our eyes with this silent meeting of June and January. No traffic passed us. No one else was there. The little dogs looked off across the ruffling blossoms, and I was dazzled. America *is* beautiful, and we had seen its many aspects, none so stunning as this snow garden at the moment when predatory seasons were at bay, their banners bright. We had reached the

Continental Divide, that ridgeline beyond which the flow is westward. Once again we were between destinations, neither of which was really home, and now we stood as visitors beside this mountain cradle, its fragile coverlet, its soft pillows immaculate. It reminded me of a perfect world within a ball of heavy glass, complete, beckoning, forever out of reach, and for a moment I was overwhelmed with my own sense of homelessness, a hollow feeling of alienation that had been growing inside me ever since we left Connecticut.

It was then that one of my dogs stood on her hind legs to reach her front paws to my knee, a way she has of reminding me that she is there and it is time to be moving on. I looked down to see both dogs looking up at me, their backs to all that beauty, their tails moving. And then I knew. Home was there beside me as it had always been, familiar and responsive, filled with the small signals of affection only a family member recognizes. I reached down, patted each round head and turned back to the car. The dogs ran ahead of me. After nearly nine thousand miles we had never left home, and my dogs had known it all along.

A Prisoner in
A Game Bird Sanctuary

At six o'clock on a Friday morning, the second day of June, I awoke to the sound of low conversation just outside my bedroom window, murmured words I couldn't quite catch, although I seemed to be the subject of discussion. I was the newly arrived visitor from California, the first occupant of the guest house by the river, and my neighbors were up and curious. Should I lie there pretending to sleep until I had been explained, or should I greet my callers, ask them in for coffee? While I decided, the mumbling grew louder, reaching me through every open window, as if an audience awaited my appearance and was growing restless. My dogs lifted their heads from the blanket to listen, their growls muffled and uncertain. Quietly I moved to the nearest window. The grassy slope between the house and the river bank was covered with ducks. I went to another window. Solid ducks between the house and my car parked under a willow tree. I opened the front door to meet the stares of three Canadian geese grazing on the violets at my doorstep. My appearance in the doorway raised the level of conversation, but not a single wing. My house was entirely surrounded by hundreds of ducks and geese, none of them discussing me. Returning to the bedroom I reassured my dogs. "You wouldn't believe it if I told you," I whispered. They dropped their chins between their paws.

While I ate my first breakfast in the guest house my dogs sat behind the front door screen looking out upon the sea of birds. They were nervous and so was I. I have never gotten along well with large, edible birds. I don't know why this is, but the gap which separates a man from a duck seems to me abysmal, and there is no getting along with a goose. Like people who are allergic to cats and who therefore find cats in their laps wherever they go, I seem to attract poultry. That morning it appeared that the ghost of every chicken I have ever eaten had returned transmogrified to dine on me.

As I pondered my next move, a hollow-sounding wind enveloped the house. It was a sound I was to hear each morning of my stay, a turbulence created by hundreds of flapping wings straining to lift fat bodies from the ground. I joined my dogs in the doorway in time to see a bearded man approaching in a cloud of birds. He was pushing a wheelbarrow, and he seemed oblivious to the flap he had stirred up. He stopped outside my house to scatter a pailful of corn on the grass. Then he pushed on, and as he passed I saw that the deep bed of his wheelbarrow was filled with cracked corn. From my kitchen window I watched him stop at a fence gate just beyond my house. Nailed to the gate was a large metal sign I hadn't noticed when we arrived the night before.

GAME BIRD SANCTUARY
           Hunting
           Fishing
NO **Horses**
           Dogs
           Bicycles

The bird feeder pushed his load through the open gate and into a pasture toward a row of trees along the river bank. I waited for him to reappear with an explanation and soon he returned behind his empty wheelbarrow, glad to accept my offer of a cup of coffee. Sandy is a slight, genial man in his late fifties whose gray beard and untrimmed hair, held back from his weathered face by a leather headband, give him the appearance of the Ancient Mariner as he fights off his flock each morning. I was living, he explained, at the edge of a game bird sanctuary established since my departure for California twenty years before. The pasture where once my horse had grazed was now a land trust, fenced and posted for the exclusive use of wild ducks and geese. A bird resort had been created along the shores and in the river. Banks had been pushed back, screened with laurel and azalea and wild rose bushes, and five small islands had been formed of bottom silt to provide nesting sites. River pools had been deepened for landing strips, and in the center of the largest pool a float was anchored for sunning and preening. Above this pond a fall of curling water offered a place for water sports.

Each morning, Sandy told me, he scattered one hndred pounds of corn along the river bank, some of it in clearings for the geese, the rest in undergrowth the ducks prefer. Between October and April a second load of corn was distributed each evening. Wild ducks and geese made up the pampered population of this playground where every whim was coddled, and so accustomed were the birds to being waited on, so impatient for an early breakfast, that they stormed ashore each morning on my side of the fence to wait for Sandy. "Don't they ever leave?" I asked him. "Why should they?" he answered, brushing a tail feather from his beard.

By the time I moved in at the edge of the bird refuge generations of geese and ducks had known no other home. Man, their tormentor, had become their slave and they were not only unafraid, they had become insistent complainers over the slightest inconvenience. For the month of June I was to become that inconvenience. My dogs and I were also to become the victims of environmental reversal, to endure an imbalance in which we stood a chance of vanishing. If my observations of the offensive creatures who so outnumbered us seem unduly subjective, they are not those of a bird watcher safe in his blind, but rather of a watched and harrassed intruder in a world where ducks are pushy and geese intolerant.

Although the ducks outnumbered the geese by ten to one in the sanctuary, the habits and character of the larger bird made a more lasting impression on me. The Canadian, or Canada, goose is classified as wild game rather than common poultry not because he is independent of man, but because he is a traveling mendicant, admired only when he is going somewhere else. His diet consists of handouts, the tail feathers of other birds and golf courses. Not surprisingly, he is often overweight. For a goose he is well dressed with the tweedy look of a country squire. His neck is as supple and strong as a vacuum cleaner hose and when angry he flexes this feathered tube. Afloat, the goose neck enables him to reach for bottom plants, to watch for tourists with cracker boxes, and, by extending his neck at water level, to become a lethal weapon. The only difference apparent to a nongoose between the male and female is the longer, thicker neck of the gander. Canadian geese have nasty, curling tongues and cheap rubber feet.

The call of the Canadian goose is a rising grind very similar to the sound of automobile brakes suddenly applied, except that it comes out of a goose not at sudden stops but at sudden starts. He hates to be interrupted. The goose, like most water fowl, is more believable afloat than on land where he does not look as if he would float at all. His hull is broad, his bottom shallow, and his landings on water are heavy. Nevertheless, in all the landings I observed the goose managed to avoid capsizing. Invariably his return to the water is followed by a rapid twitching of tail feathers, the goose's way of thumbing his nose at those of us who were hoping he would sink.

Canadian geese are strict parents who literally keep their offspring in line. A goose family I watched turned outings on the river into naval maneuvres, the father in front, the mother an exact distance behind, the six goslings evenly spaced between. Never did a gosling drift out of formation. Rest stops ashore were also organized. While the parents stood watch, the six young geese bunched and followed orders. If one sat down, all sat down; if one scratched his ear, all scratched their ears. When I arrived the goslings were the size of fryers, all a neutral shade of brown. When I left they were half grown, fully feathered and undergoing flight trials. Still they stayed in line. No wonder geese are paranoid.

During my stay the duck population grew steadily. New arrivals registered every day and, according to Sandy, twenty-five hundred made it for the winter season. Although the flock included pintails, wood and black ducks, mallards made up the huge majority and looked exactly like decoys. For some reason, ducks prefer breakfast in the bushes. They also refused to lay eggs on those man-made islands. After one precarious inspection, I would have too. The duck personality is totally unlike the goose's. Ducks don't take themselves seriously, and I certainly can't blame them for that.

They spend most of the day pretending to swim without kicking their feet, sailing around in circles like bathtub toys. When heavy rain emptied the pond of geese, the ducks remained, and water does roll off their backs. It is the ducks who ride the waterfall, who pinch each other's bottoms for a laugh, then laugh.

The configuration of a duck on take-off from the water reminded me of the Concorde jet, neck stiff, bill down, tail dragging. Getting a duck up looks to be as difficult as lifting a snake. Like geese, they are graceful on the water and in the air. It is getting from one to the other that is clumsy and uncertain.

Ducks are permissive parents. They part company, leaving the mother with a batch of eggs she never ordered. I watched a family of mother and thirteen ducklings and marvelled at her nonchalance. Her children were all over the pond, but she sailed on playing the Duck. Ducks also mumble. It was this sound I heard on my first morning, and, while I stopped trying to figure out their remarks, I could never ignore the implications. They also yawn a lot, or at least they did around me. The worst thing about the ducks I lived with, though, was their number. While even a single goose is too many, a couple of ducks are decorative. Hundreds filling the pond and overflowing its banks on flat, red paddles, their eyes as expressionless as studs, are sanctimonious.

It was the landing of this feathered host which made me a prisoner in my own house. They stepped ashore at dawn, surging up the slope toward level ground, ducks and geese intermixed, until they covered every foot between my front door and the barn where the corn was stored. So relentless was their march that I saw a squirrel, sitting erect one moment with a corn kernel between its paws, disappear the next in a tide of birds.

Sandy's appearance at the barn door was the breakfast call, and birds swooped toward him. Flinging corn around was, I realized, a matter of self defense. Without a handout he never would have made it to the gate.

To venture beyond my door before mid-morning was impossible. My dogs tried it first, dashing into the flock without a qualm. Used to routing peacocks at home, they consider all birds flighty. But as soon as they had dispatched a cloud of birds in one direction, another regiment moved in, leaving them stranded. I made a path through the birds to rescue the dogs, only to find them both in the river where they had followed a duck without stopping at the bank. Back we came to the house, kicking our way through ducks, going around geese, and there we stayed until the main body of birds had followed Sandy down river. It just wasn't worth it.

Between mid-morning and early afternoon I was left almost alone to walk by the river, to sit on the bank with a book. This was a quiet time in a postcard scene, the parenthetic pond reflecting deep foliage and a cloudless sky, only the willow leaves moving on the water's surface betraying the undercurrent. Shortly after one o'clock each afternoon two neon-colored ducks appeared, moving upstream while pretending they were only drifting. I looked up from a page to admit how well they fitted into the pond scene. A paragraph later two more ducks arrived. Slowly then the pond filled until its surface disappeared. Then came the geese like sailing ships among canoes, taking over the float, causing collisions. Finally, the goose family came ashore, making straight for me. My day by the river ended.

All the birds came ashore in late afternoon to graze. Now the flock was torpid, fat bodies tilted toward blades of grass they only gummed. This second landing was in some ways worse than the first, however, because the birds were even less inclined to make room for us. Not even the dogs could stir them into flight, and a goose or two usually stood at the screen door to watch us. It is a belittling experience to face a goose at the door when the law is on his side.

Evenings at the edge of the sanctuary were my favorite time of day. On the opposite bank a muskrat lived in a water pocket formed by the parted roots of a sapling. I watched for his appearance, a furtive peek for patrolling geese, then a nose moving steadily across the pond. At the muskrat's signal insects pricked the water and now and then a fish jumped, then flopped back with an evening meal. The pond was no longer a landing strip, and as it came to life, so did I, our freedom flag a muskrat's nose.

In the final days of my visit a strange thing happened. I began to feel sorry for the birds. They were wild, but I was free. I would migrate, not they. Paunched and protected, they had lost the will to travel. They were the prisoners after all. Where breakfast is served in a wheelbarrow and the nesting is easy, the result is sanctuary sprawl and a gradual stiffening of wing joints.

But then, you can't explain that to a goose.

The Noninterruptibles

The Office of Preparedness has admitted to the existence of an ultrasecret list of officials and other essential citizens to be saved in the event of cataclysmic disaster. Those selected will be whisked through tunnels to buried chambers where their survival is assured. They are called "the noninterruptibles."

Ever since man first looked up, then down from his viewpoint midway between the reptile and the bird he has been curious about the creatures fashioned before him. From fossil remains to vestigial tails he has imagined a chain of life painfully making its way toward the perfection of himself, a production line in which new and improved models replace old, in which skeletal junkyards litter the biosphere and the Edsels of nature are quickly discarded. He has looked backward with smug appreciation of his own remarkable design and forward with contented conviction that he, like the Volkswagon, is just about perfect the way he is.

If his satisfaction with his own original conception is justified, it is not the first time nature has hit upon perfection on the first try. There are other examples still functioning well. The scorpion, for instance, which predates the dinosaur by several million years, turned out to be right the first time. On the other hand, the tortoise, tiptoeing like Oliver Hardy toward unsuspected disaster, is not working out. His is convincing proof that when you attempt to take it with you, you don't always get there.

While geologists, anthropologists and zoo keepers cooperate to confirm the ascendency of man by showing us how far we have come, biologists and physicists are working hard to assure us that we still have far to go. Here, however, the ground becomes shakier. Carbon dating tells us how old we are, but not how old we will be. Our anticipation span, as our reckless gambling with our own future testifies, extends barely half a century, seldom stretching far enough to include the welfare of our children's grandchildren. Unlike all else in nature we have the minds and the thumbs to leave our mark, to force the rest of life to adapt itself to us rather than the reverse. Millenia from now we will be able to prove we were here. But to whom?

I think I have an idea. Despite the proven durability of several older forms of life and the mastery of men over nearly every species, there is one small animal whose mastery of man continues unshaken. He is a creature with more natural enemies than friends, with fewer chances for survival in the open than a mouse, yet he thrives. He has inspired more human ingenuity to exterminate him than even the house fly. He is bombed and poisoned, bulldozed and missled, flooded out and walled in. Still, in this century of successful reduction of all nonhuman life to manageable numbers, the gopher is alive and well and usually dies in his bed. Moreover, his battles of wits are being won in our own backyards.

I pride myself on being a live-and-let-live man who opens doors to allow insects to escape, who rescues mangled mice from my cat, who bears no malice toward the coinhabitants of my sphere. My confrontation with gophers, however, has undermined my altruism. That we like the same things should establish common bonds. It does not, because what I believe should grow up, the gopher thinks should grow down. We look at the world from opposite directions as the common ground between us sinks slowly toward the gopher.

The North American pocket gopher is the same gopher the Greeks named Thomomys, or "heap mouse." The French call him *gaufre*, or "honeycomb," and we spell his name our own way. He has fur-lined cheeks with slits in them for easy filling, and as soon as his pockets bulge he retires to one of several storerooms where he not only empties his cheeks but turns them inside out to clean them. Gophers do not tolerate pocket lint. All evidence to the contrary, gophers are solitary animals who meet only to mate and who otherwise live out their lives as single occupants of their underground mansions. These contain several bedrooms, storerooms and bathrooms connected by long hallways reaching as far as five hundred feet from the cenral rooms, and to insure privacy the passageways are so narrow that two gophers coming from opposite directions cannot pass each other.

Gophers dig with their front teeth, and nature, who thought of everything when she designed the gopher, equipped him with very thin lips which he compresses into a tight smile to keep the dirt out of his mouth. His lifespan is four years, and old age is common because the gopher never displays more than half of himself to anyone else. This not only makes him difficult to catch, but also to identify. (Minnesota calls itself the Gopher State in the mistaken impression that its striped ground squirrels and prairie dogs are gophers.) Gophers can run backward as easily as forward and can somersault in their one-way tunnels. These few advantages have proven to be quite sufficent.

With few exceptions gophers like everything we like, and it is in the division of our mutual bounty that we have disagreed. Our energetic counterattacks have produced profits for industry but few dead gophers. Abetted by gopher snakes, weasels, badgers, owls, cats and almost every other predator, we still have failed. Undaunted we continue the fight, certain that there is no force on earth equal to an aroused citizenry. Undiminished, the gopher pops half way up now and then to see how we are doing.

Where gophers thrive the number of home remedies is inexhaustible. Each year wherever people gather to discuss the weather and Washington someone discloses the latest device for ridding the world of gophers, and I have often been present when such confidences are shared. Like an overheard stock tip, a gopher cure attracts listeners, the room becomes silent as we heed the expert. At a Beverly Hills party a man from Oregon told us about a gopher bush, a shrub so revolting to gophers that any garden is safe for yards around it. He promised each of us a cutting, and in time my sample arrived by fourth-class mail disguised as printed matter to avoid confiscation. The cutting was already lifeless by the time it reached me. Delivery time had taken two weeks.

Last spring a neighbor of mine tried smog. A wiry gopherphobe, she attached a garden hose to the tailpipe of her car, then backed the car around her lawn, stopping near each gopher hole long enough to fill the passage with toxic gasses, but the cross ventilation built into gopher tunnels quickly dispelled the fumes, and her gopher soon covered her lawn with new mounds of topsoil. An avid vegetable grower in a nearby town sent out word that by planting jalapeña peppers at the four corners of a garden gophers would stay away. I tried this, adding several extra pepper plants along the exposed sides of my small patch of tomatoes, beets and carrots. As soon as the small plants were well up, they began to disappear one by one, pulled down into gopherland. Except, of course, the jalapeñas. They grew to maturity, and by mid-August I harvested a small basket of peanut-size peppers too hot for man or gopher.

Again this spring an ingenious gopher solution was proposed. According to country gossip, the latest surefire gopher chaser is a collection of empty quart bottles sunk into the ground on the windward side of the garden so that the open mouths of the bottles are flush with the ground and slightly tilted. Theory has it that any breeze stirring across the bottle tops will create an ominous whistling sound intolerable to the sensitive ears of gophers. Whoever discovered this flaw in the otherwise perfect gopher has not revealed himself in any of my scientific journals, but in unending wars weapons must be tested in the field.

I had already decided not to plant anything except in reinforced redwood tubs this year, so I took no action on the bottle cure, but a friend of mine, an intrepid gardner, decided to try it to protect his new rows of lettuce, zucchini and green beans. He buried empty bottles along the northwest slope of his garden where the afternoon breezes circulate. Then he waited, his hopes high, his faith strong. I visited him soon to see for myself how things were going. It was a windless evening and no audible sound came from the bottles. "You'll have to create a night wind," I told him, "or else train an owl to whistle."

"I'm working on that," he answered, but he was not amused.

On my second visit to his patch a few weeks later I

found him in a high state of nervousness. We visited the vegetables just before dark where I understood immediately the reason for his battle fatigue. The garden was now brightly lighted by floodlights strung on wires from the house to the nearest tree. A fine-mesh wire fence surrounded the vegetables and had been sunk four feet below ground level. Two electric fans whirred back and forth across the open bottle tops, creating a sound audible only to gophers.

A few days later my friend called me, a defeated man. It seems that he had gone out of town for two days, making it necessary to turn off fans and floodlights for two nights. When he returned he found most of his vegetables gone, although he did say his gopher seemed to prefer bibb lettuce to zucchini. The significant evidence of a superior intelligence at work, however, lay in his row of bottles. Each had been partially filled with loose soil pushed up from new gopher tunnels.

Another gopher fighter has surrendered. Another gopher has filled his reversible cheek pouches and retired to the comforts of his underground larder. The battle goes on, but the victor has been proclaimed. Perhaps occasional defeat is good for us. Humility before the half gopher we see may steady us and save us from ourselves.

If not, and our mad course continues to its destructive climax, a day when the earth can no longer support even the gopher, he will have already prepared an alternate exit to a more hospitable star.

The Spirit of May is Blithe

May is the month of poets and meadowlarks. On the first day of May a lark I know deposited four eggs in a grass bowl in a corner of my pasture. Not being blithe, I worried about them. According to the program for larks, weaving a nest of grass on the first of May is the thing to do, and a pasture corner is the place. The sun is warm by mid-morning; the grass is high, and the summer banquet is endless. Except that for centuries larks have been building grass houses in the wrong places, then getting upset about it. Shakespeare called the lark the ploughman's clock, and no wonder. It goes off everytime we ploughmen walk through our fields.

I belong to the race of lark startlers. Morning after morning I have startled this lark into flapping, floating flight, her high cries strident and resentful. "It is the lark that sings so out of tune," but only out of our tune. When this lark rose silently on the first day of May to drop again into the grass a few feet in front of me, I knew one of us had changed. When I saw the eggs inches from an irrigation pipe I had just set down, I knew which of us it was.

Few of nature's beginnings demand more cooperation from an uncooperative world than a lark's egg. There it sits on the surface of the earth, small and white and flecked with brown, not fooling anybody. It is underfoot where no egg should be. These lark's eggs were within the radius of rainbirds, and if spring irrigation was to continue, the nest by evening would be drenched. "The lark leaves his watery nest," Old Sir William D'Avenant wrote, "and climbing shakes his dewy wings." But not that watery! Not that dewy!

My decision made, I picked up my pipes and moved on, leaving the nest dry, the pasture around it withering. My cooperation was only to be expected because I am a man, but not all who travel pasture paths read Shakespeare and Shelley. There are, for instance, three horses with twelve feet, each larger than a lark's nest. I watched from my window as they moved into the lark's territory, then ran to the pasture to drive them away. They heard my shout, "Look out, lark's nest!" then went back to brunch. When I arrived at the nest the lark rose from the grass under the horses' noses. I was the only threat.

For the rest of May, while others planned weddings and vacations, while the nights were bright with midnight moons and the days heavy with the toasted smell of newly cut hay, I worried about the lark's eggs. And I became convinced that the instinct for self-multiplication present in larks and some others thrives without reason. The odds against those eggs hatching grew with the calendar. The chance that one egg would remain unbroken, that one new lark would sing at Heaven's gate this summer grew chancier each morning.

Still the nest and eggs went undisturbed. Then my six heifers found the corner and moved in for midday siestas. As I watched, they settled in a circle around the nest. (Cows settle in three sections and rise in two, an indication, perhaps, of how a cow feels at the end of a nap.) I expected scrambled lark's eggs.

I approached the dozing calves slowly, careful not to startle them. They saw me out of half-closed eyes, their jaws revolving, their interest in me negligible. As I stood just outside their circle, the lark rose from its center, once again because of me. She felt safe in a circle of six four-hundred-pound nest crushers, unsafe in the presence of one worried man. I went home to stay.

Some of us continue to worry about the fragility of our world, our fears for the end of unending life growing. But not all. Not a meadowlark in a circle of calves.

Immortal Hari

When Hari and I first met he was a refugee, the youngest victim of the Bel-Air fire which all but destroyed that well-known community of mansions nestled in the expensive California tinder next to Beverly Hills. His owner, a famous musician and friend of mine, called me the morning after being driven from his burning house to temporary quarters in an apartment building beyond the fire zone where dogs and children, even if otherwise homeless, were not allowed. Would I keep Hari until his house was rebuilt, perhaps six months? All I knew then about Hari was that he was a puppy whose breed I had never heard of, that only a few weeks ago he had been the centerpiece in the window of a Beverly Hills pet store when my friend passed by. He was not shopping for a dog, but he could not pass the window. That much information suggested that Hari must have been expensive, that he must also be irresistible. With a family already including collies and cats, of course I agreed to keep Hari for as long as necessary.

Late that afternoon Hari and his owner, connected by a new leash, were waiting for me on the sidewalk in front of their dogless apartment building. I must have greeted my friend, sympathized with his misfortune, but all I remember of our fateful meeting was the black-and-white puppy I lifted into my arms, the smell of smoke on his fur, the warmth of his fat body as he wriggled toward my face to lick the tip of my nose. All puppies are instant charmers, not only because they are helpless, heedless, headlong companions of the best and worst of us, but because without exception their disproportionate dimensions remind us of our own babies. Heads are a little too large, faces a little too small, torsoes a little too long, limbs a little too short. These are features puppies and babies share, and puppies have an added smile, a tail.

Lhasa Apsos are a Tibetan breed that never quite adjusts to adult canine proportions. The Lhasa grows up all wrong in all the right places. His round head is always too large; his face never develops a profile; his stubby legs support a long, low body at a slant. This forward tilt is exaggerated by a high plume tail set backwards, like a tea kettle handle, and because his face is already close to the ground he lies down from front to back. All of these permanent puppy features are later overlaid with a cape of long, silken hair, parted along his spine, falling forward to his button nose. He moves as if he were making his way out from under a blanket.

Hari was not only the epitome of puppies, he was also a Lhasa. He may have been designed by God, but he could have been designed by Disney.

Preparing my family for Hari's emergency visit was easy. All were used to animals as natural family members, to be considered and respected, to be reprimanded and forgiven, to be loved, not possessed.

Much more difficult for me was explaining to my three daughters that Hari was a temporary guest until his own house was rebuilt. Each assured me she understood, pleased to rescue any victim of the holocaust that had come so close to our own house. But, of course, that was before Hari and I arrived. When I carried him through the kitchen door, removed his leash and allowed him to precede me into the swarm of cats and collies and little girls waiting to welcome him, saw him fling his tail over his back, as Lhasas do when they prepare to meet the world head on, then march purposefully into their midst, I knew that Hari would be much more than a houseguest. He would be king.

And by the end of that first evening Hari had chosen his queen. My oldest daughter Susie was then twelve, but because she was born with a rare and incurable bone disease, one of whose symptoms was brittle bones easily and often broken, she could not enjoy the company of collies. Also, as a result of Susie's affliction she was tiny, never weighing more than sixty pounds, and usually confined to a wheelchair. She had lived her life surrounded by a family of large, healthy people and animals, never wondering, aloud at least, whether there was anyone small enough to ride beside her in her chair, to sleep at the foot of her bed without crushing her, anyone willing to accept her limited world as big enough if she was also there. That night there was, and he was Hari.

Hari wasted no time reorganizing our family according to his own priorities. His first concern was Susie to whom he was immediately devoted. He rode with her, sat under the piano bench while she practiced, ran into her room every few minutes between his other duties to check up on her. Susie's research revealed that one of the traditional roles of these Tibetan dogs was to warm the toes of the Lamas in that mountainous region where temperatures are low and royal toes cold. Apparently, Hari's brief life in California had not disrupted his genetic discipline, and whenever Susie's toes were available he rested his chin across them. Next on his list of the favored were my wife and I, large providers, family catalysts whom Hari counted as necessary. My younger daughters were acknowledged because they were also humans, the only species Hari considered worthy of his attention, but because they were occupied with cats and kangaroo rats, objects Hari did not find amusing, he wagged his tail in passing, no more. As for the collies, he treated them as members of a lower order, harmless enough but certainly not like him. Only when they forgot their place outside and attempted to join the rest of us did Hari warn them off. All of these responsibilities kept him busy, for someone was always out of Hari's order, or if not, the doorbell rang. Lhases have voices much larger than they are, and if heard and not seen they are effective watch dogs.

And of course Hari grew. According to his breed, he did so horizontally, seeming to sink toward the floor as he grew longer. His coat spread over his body until only his tail remained the reliable indication of which end was which. Perhaps to give his front end character, his lower canines jutted over his upper lip, bulldog style, so that facing him nose to nose reminded me of a confrontation with a drill sergeant whose tail wagged.

As the weeks of Hari's visit passed, Susie's life changed. Always enthusiastic, interested in a wide range of activities she could only read about, her high spirits now fairly bubbled. Instead of other people's adventures, our discussions each evening now concerned her own accounts of Hari's progress toward perfection. Every paragraph of her report began with "Hari and I." Every concluding opinion was "Don't you think that was smart of him?" She consulted and praised him, defended and forgave him. She needed other company less often, and never minded being left alone. She'd be fine. Hari was there.

I watched this mutual commitment with increasing anxiety. I could no longer bring myself to mention Hari's other family, nor could Susie. Occasionally, I met with owner, who invariably began our conversation with "How's Hari?" to which I quickly countered "How's the house coming along?" Neither of us ever answered the other's question. And although our work together had always been collaboration I enjoyed, I began to dread our meetings. Weeks turned into months, winter became spring, as Southern California seasons imperceptibly become each other, and Susie's world remained the sunlit kingdom where she and Hari lived.

Then the telephone call. "We're back in the house," he told me, then paused. "But why don't you keep Hari. After all, he's lived almost all his life with you."

I must have protested softly. I don't remember now. I do remember running into Susie's room. "They don't want Hari back. He's yours."

And her response. She reached for Hari's round head as he lay beside her. "How could anybody not want Hari?"

The years of Hari's life with Susie are difficult to separate into the changing rhythms of their partnership, the small crests and troughs they rode together as Susie lived through her teens and Hari his middle age. I do remember one recurring crisis: Hari developed a chronic itch, a skin condition common, I was told, to Lhasas in semi-tropic climates. Periodically he was taken to the veterinarian to be shaved so that air and medication could reach his inflamed skin. At such times he came home wearing only eyebrows and a tuft at the end of his tail, a ridiculous costume for such a dog. He looked like a random assortment, not the sum of his parts, but neither he nor Susie seemed to notice. And his coat grew in glossier than ever until he was once again well hidden. Also, as he grew older he lost several small front teeth, releasing the tip of his tongue to add a touch of color to his pugnacious expression.

Certainly, the high point of those years was Hari's marriage, arranged, conducted and paid for by Susie. By the time she decided that Hari needed a wife Lhasas had become celebrities at dog shows and in households where they replaced toy poodles as pampered pets. They were still rare enough to be expensive, however, and it required all of Susie's savings and a trip to Bakersfield to find a bride for Hari. She named the golden puppy Dalai after the Lama whose toes were warmed by Lhasas, and wedding preparations were begun as soon as Hari exhibited more than casual interest in his bride-to-be. They were married at Susie's bedside in a ceremony complete with vows and stern reminders of marital responsibility. Hari listened attentively as always to every word Susie spoke, wagging at one end, snorting his doubts at the other. Dalai seemed distracted, but both dogs shared Susie equally. Each trusted her completely.

In the sixth year of Hari's life he became the father of a small replica of himself, a female Susie named Tibetsi, born under her bed. Once again we were reminded that Lhasa puppies belong at the tops of Christmas stockings. Tibetsi was to become the image of Hari, large for a female, fearlessly agressive, scornful of all non-humans and subject to Hari's itch. One difference which became important to me was her willingness to switch allegiance from Susie to the rest of us, and soon she was accompanying me and my youngest daughter to a small ranch where we spent our weekends raising Angus calves and a colt for riding. Susie allowed the puppy to go with us to the country, but she would not allow Hari to go along. "Hari is not a cowboy," she reminded me. "He's a palace dog."

Our ranch beyond all city limits was intended as a family alternative to city confinement, a place where each of us could live two days a week free of fence and ordinance. There we could walk without connecting leashes, dig a hole or climb a tree or pick a flower that belonged to no one. Instead, this refuge divided us. The relentless progress of Susie's disease made trips to the country impossible for her. Half of us, including Hari, remained in the city; half, including collies and a younger daughter took off on Friday to attend our growing country family. Hari by then was eight years old, his ways were set, and the natural world of interdependent species had never interested him. Even his concession to the undeniable need to go outside he made with mutterings of protest.

At last, however, Hari was given no choice. Susie's condition had always required periodic visits to the hospital where she received blood transfusions and antibiotics to slow the debilitating progress of her disease. As she grew older, these hospital stays became more frequent and in her twentieth year often lasted several weeks. And because the most effective antidote had always been her high spirits, her enthusiasm for every aspect of her life, these confinements must not be allowed to diminish her sense of participation in our lives. Accordingly, her mother moved into the hospital with her to provide company and conversation, special treats and special love, above all to give Susie the sense of belonging to her family. Hari, of course, was not allowed to visit her, but on more than one occasion he was smuggled into her hospital room, gift wrapped to look like an expensive toy, a scarf tied under his chin, his nose and radiating petals of fur too perfect to be the face of a real dog. But now there was no one to take care of him on weekends, so with Susie's agreement Hari and his family joined us in the country.

Hari went about reorganizing another household with his usual fervor, but its members were even larger and were scattered over seven acres of corrals and outbuildings and impenetrable vegetation. With Dalai and her puppy tagging along, Hari's weekends were exhausting efforts to locate and sort out everybody. Wherever he went he was confronted with large faces staring into his, with badger burrows deep enough to swallow him, with burrs and thistles that collected in his coat until he was immobilized.

My reports to Susie at the end of these weekends were vitally important to her. Had Hari enjoyed himself? Had he met any interesting friends? Did I bear in mind that he was born to warm the toes of Lamas, not to dig for gophers? My Sunday evening accounts of Hari's country adventures were edited to reassure her that her dog's behavior was impeccable, that his bravery in the face of an Angus steer was matched only by his canny decision to let beef with horns and hooves alone. I left her reassured, proud of Hari's expanding talents as a ranch hand, never surprised to discover that he was a surprising dog.

Susie's twentieth birthday was celebrated in November at her hospital bedside with Hari in attendance. It was an occasion made more festive by her doctor's promise that she would be home for Christmas, and preparations were begun in the early weeks of December for that happy event. For my part, I made arrangements to bring a Christmas tree from the country, a special tree cut from the high slopes of the mountains surrounding our ranch. The weekend before the holiday the tree was delivered in a pickup truck driven by a friend unaware of Hari's habit of challenging all arrivals. Before I could head him off Hari ran under the wheels of the truck. The driver never saw him. We rushed him to a veterinarian, but his life ended in that awful moment before my eyes. We buried him that morning in a grove of pines, a sacred place where in later years other members of our animal family have joined him, victims of no-fault accidents faultless behavior never quite explains.

Later that day I reached my wife at the hospital. "We mustn't tell Susie," we told each other with no idea how to keep her from knowing. The following morning, a Sunday, I was called again. Susie's doctor, an eminent bone specialist and devoted friend of hers, had firmly warned that her precarious hold on life might slip if she were told of Hari's death. Somehow Hari must be kept alive so that Susie would want to live.

In the days and weeks that followed I was assisted to some extent in my deception. Susie's condition had so deteriorated that she was unable to leave, except for brief periods, the life-supporting paraphenalia hospitals provide. She did come home for Christmas, but only for the day, and it was reasonable, she agreed, that Hari and the rest of the animals remain in the country. Also, we had sold our city house and moved to an apartment nearer the hospital, a necessary reduction in expenses and responsibilities, and while small pets were allowed in the building, our ark of animals would never have been tolerated there. The ranch was now their home, as it was becoming mine, and Susie felt as we all did, that Hari should never become an apartment dog, forced to adjust to a world of elevators and parking lots, foul smelling pet areas and thin-walled cubicles where a bark was grounds for eviction.

It became necessary for me to divide my time equally between the country and city families in order to fulfill responsibilities in both places. I spent three successive weekdays at the apartment, while a country neighbor took care of the animals, then four days at the ranch with my youngest daughter. Susie and her mother remained together at home or in the hospital. The arrangement was manageable, if never entirely satisfactory, and it did account for Hari's continuing absence. Nothing could make easy my regular arrivals at Susie's bedside, however, when news of Hari was her first request. Making up stories to delight a child is a precious part of every parent's experience, but relating Hari's fictitious adventures to a perceptive twenty-year-old who knew him far better than I was the most difficult task I have ever undertaken. Knowing the possible consequences of my failure to be convincing made those performances less, rather than more credible, for an actor, which I am not, must believe his lines. Fortunately, Hari's wife and daughter thrived on country life, and their experiences became his. I told of encounters with peacocks and kittens, of trips to the dump and excursions to gather wildflowers. The country air would be good for Hari's itch, Susie decided. "It's more like Tibet up there." My throat tightened and I could not answer.

I was called upon to keep Hari alive and well for nine months. To say that I succeeded would be to overestimate my skills and to underestimate my daughter's sensitive awareness. Although she gave no indication that she suspected the truth, toward the end of her life she asked less often about Hari. I am certain this was partly to spare me, for Susie's concern for the slightest discomfort she detected in the rest of us was always greater than her worries about herself. And she was blessed with that sixth sense the handicapped share, insight unrelated to the physical receptors that guide the rest of us, reserved for those who need it most. I believe she knew. I also believe that the truth did not upset her so drastically as we believed it might. For her Hari was there beside her where he belonged.

I realize now that my attempts to give Hari a life beyond his own were never necessary. He had taken care of that, as he took care of all his responsibilities to Susie. He was never one to leave a doubt about his presence, but he believed that the larger we were the more we needed reminding. Just in case, his daughter with all his ways rests her chin lightly on my toes today. Even that was an unnecessary precaution. Hari is immortal. He always was.

In Other Words

On a morning in April when the clocks were all wrong, when the sky at four A.M was the color of old iron, not the basic black the clocks said it should be, I had this dream. In it I was making my way home through rising flood waters, crawling along the crumbling banks of swollen streams, slipping into swirling brown currents against which I struggled toward a stilted hillside house, my unfamiliar home. Suddenly, the air around me was filled with desperate cries for help, a strident chorus of high voices screaming to be saved, so near that the cries awakened me. As the dream scene faded, the shrill sounds grew louder. My house was once again surrounded by invisible peacocks balanced on fence posts, tree stumps, any pedestal, begging to be rescued from the obliterating half-light in which even peacocks vanish.

Acknowledgment was immediate. My collie was the first to reply with a bark that indicated he was not interested. Animal voices that only annoy him draw a deeper sound than he would use to greet a visiting dog. His comment was loud enough, however, to raise an answering yelp from a farmhouse half a mile away. My two smaller dogs joined him then at the open bedroom window to pour cascades of blurry warnings into the discussion. When they are not sure of their target they use a buckshot language designed to reach anyone within range. The peacocks were answered next by my neighbor's rooster, his crow now a footnote instead of the headline it was meant to be. Finally, two cats, awakened by the uproar, clashed with such piercing hatred that all the rest fall silent.

Later, much later, the sky lightened. The tremulous conversation of small birds in the pines began. The inflammatory speeches were over, and the gossip was idle. My old cat chirped at the door to be let out. The frog in my windowbox delivered a bronchial comment. A horse at the fence ahemmed.

The animal world is noisy with announcements. Lobsters creak, crabs rattle, even clams snap. Fish grunt, rabbits shriek, mice sing. It comes as something of a relief to learn that storks and pelicans are mute, as are most reptiles. (Only the white man, not the snake, speaks with forked tongue.) To the underwater listener a coral reef sounds like a barnyard, and dolphin double-talk is bedlam. Everyone who moves makes use of sound, and almost everyone has something to say. What each species is talking about, if anything at all, whether all the talk is intended to persuade or is merely a compulsive urge to sound off, have recently become subjects for speculation among biologists and others not so certain as they once were that language is exclusively ours, the gift that makes us human.

What prompts animals to speak? One theory is that the topics of conversation are limited to sex, diet, possible threat to survival and occasionally the weather, subjects most likely to be discussed at any cocktail party. Which of these, if any, concerned the peacocks who awakened me? On moonlit winter nights we often hear the high-pitched voices of coyotes as they move to lower ground in search of food. To me they sound like children in a schoolyard, outshouting each other with careless joy. On mornings when the fog lowers the sky to treetop level flocks of starlings fill the live oaks until every twig squeaks with conversation. Are they really speaking of serious matters? Late on a recent sunny afternoon a cat I call the watch cat lay asleep along the roof edge. A bluejay landed near him, hopped closer and began to scold. The jay's harsh words awoke the cat who raised his head to look over his shoulder at the jay. The cat flicked his tail once at the chattering bird, then resumed his nap. The jay flew off. Could there be a plainer example of interspecific communication?

Because the vocal apparatus in all but a few animals limits the range of sounds they are capable of making, no true animal language is believed to exist. And even where vocabulary is highly developed, animal brains are thought to be unable to produce the signals of conceptual expression. Animal talk is automatic response, like a teddy bear's squeak, not an exchange of ideas, although those who believe this admit to a wide and subtle variety of silent signals between members of the same species, communication imperceptible to us. Is this not also language? Is it not possible that we were given the ability to speak our minds as compensation for our being unable to wag our tails, wiggle our ears, or raise our hair in warning?

One barrier to animal conversation, it has been suggested, is their lack of self-awareness. They don't even know what they look like. I stood the other morning behind my old cat facing a full length mirror. I called her name, a sound she always responds to by looking at me. Instead, she met my mirrored eyes, alert as always to my reason for speaking to her. If my reflection in the mirror was to her the equivalent of me, could she have failed to recognize herself in the glass? The facing face on the surface of a pond is not a stranger's face. If it were, few animals would dare to drink.

Because animals lack true language they do not lie. Language is the mask, as well as the window of the mind, and other animals, we assume, say what they mean. But all animals deceive, an ancient matter of survival, and once again language is not always spoken, nor is it the only medium for the deceiver. Self-deception, on the other hand, requires a wide vocabulary.

Another theory: Animals speak only in the present tense. Concerned as we believe they are only with survival, the past and possible future do not occupy their thoughts or their expressions of them. They neither fantasize nor reflect; they lack metaphor. They never use the subjunctive verb form, consider the remote or propose the unlikely. Of course, this human conclusion must be based upon our observation of their behavior, not our comprehension of their signals, action serving always as the loudspeaker for those who cannot understand the words. Again, I find this somewhat arrogant assumption open to question. What prompts the small yips my dogs utter when they dream? My collie, like others of his breed, is a talker, and often for no reason apparent to me. Are his comments triggered by anticipation, memory, or are they simply a collie's response to feeling fine, like my whistling? (I always whistle in the present tense.) Are the greetings between old friends devoid of past association, whether audible or not? Are those last sighs we sigh as we settle for the night after an exciting day without their trace of backward satisfaction? Science shouts its convictions, whispers its doubts, and I am left to wonder.

I decided to conduct an experiment. One of the most intriguing of all animal sounds is the purr of a cat. It is a sound we enjoy, a voluntary expression of pleasure from the most discriminating of animals, a sound of ecstasy, of gratification. A cat's purr immediately precedes or follows a service rendered, and while it may not be intended to be heard, much less understood, we draw our own conclusions. It is fair to say, at least, that purring is an audible message from a satisfied cat and that it is the one nonhuman sound we find easiest to interpret. In fact, if we could purr we would.

But does a solitary cat purr? Without the imminent prospect of gratification of cat desire does a cat offer a purr to herself? If so, imagine the possibilities for speculation! A cat in solitude, neither hungry nor in pain, neither seeking nor responding to service, awake but neither tempted nor threatened: Would a cat in such circumstances purr? If so, could the purr be anything but contemplative? I have heard of no such experiment, and while one may have been conducted, its conclusions drawn and dutifully reported, I decided to make my own attempt to find out. I have the perfect subject, a cat I have served for fifteen years, a cat with more reason than most to purr in retrospect.

I prepared for my Spontaneous Purr Test according to what I considered to be procedure certain to produce indisputable results either way. To inspire the purr I wanted to hear, a reflective purr, the cat must be studied for at least an hour during a period when her mind can wander idly up and down her long life. I know my cat's habits, so the choice of time and place was easy. After her midday snack she retreats to a barrel-shaped rocking chair in the unused front room of my house. The chair faces a west window and is warmed by the afternoon sun. This is also the time when the dogs and I retire to my bedroom for a nap, and there is no sound in the house. The old cat settles in the chair facing the sun, her front paws tucked across her chest, her eyes half open. There she remains until we all meet again. The upholstered contours of the chair form the sort of enclosure used to isolate singers in a recording studio to screen out the sound of the instrumentalists. Whatever her thoughts, if expressed at all I would be able to record them.

I have a cassette recorder about the size of a box of Whisker Lickens, small enough to fit beside her in the chair seat without crowding her. I inserted a cartridge which records for sixty minutes without reversing the reels, waited until she was settled, then placed the machine next to her head. I must admit I felt somewhat sneaky. Any invasion of privacy is anathema to me, but, like all invaders, I convinced myself that the intrusion was in the cat's best interests. She was contributing to science, perhaps giving all cats the respect they deserve.

After my nap I returned to the chair where I found the cat in the same position. I retrieved the recorder, rewound the tape and sat down to listen. Minutes of amplified silence passed. Once I heard a low fluttering sound which I interpreted as ear scratching. Later, a series of small clicks indicated that she was either smacking her lips or licking her left front paw. (For some reason yet to be thoroughly studied, my cat washes both sides of her face with her left forepaw.) But there was no purr sound on the tape. The sounds I did hear satisfied me that if she had purred I would have recorded it, so there was nothing to do but repeat the experiment the following afternoon. After all, Konrad Lorenz needed more than a day to decipher the mating habits of jackdaws. Jane Goodall lived for years with her apes. The least I could do was give my cat a little leeway for her stroll down memory lane.

It was the fourth day's recording that produced a definite purr. The soft, throbbing sound unique to cats and Rolls Royces was unmistakable. I replayed the second or two it lasted, certain that I was listening to an unprovoked, utterly spontaneous, reminiscent purr. There was complete silence on either side of the purr, which occurred midway in tape. No outside stimulus could have inspired it. Then, I asked myself, what did?

My purr-test results may do little to refute the published assertions by scientists with impressive credentials that animals think and speak of things of immediate importance to them. Until we learn their languages, or teach them to think in ours, we draw our conclusions from autopsies, from imperfectly understood behavior, and from that old unreliable ally, human reason. Reflection and conjecture, often inaudible, are not to be discovered by such methods. But solitude is fertile soil for thinking. People and porcupines talk to themselves. So, perhaps, do cats.

In the meantime, no one shall deny me my own conclusions, nor my cat her reflective purr.

A Morning Walk with Darwin

On a recent frosty morning, refreshed after an evening dip into Darwin and a good night's sleep, I decided to follow the great naturalist's example by observing my family of animals as a biologist might observe his laboratory specimens, not as family members, that is, but as pieces of an intriguing evolutionary puzzle. I intended to identify if I could their catalog of inherited instincts, their fixed responses predetermined by their separate genetic pools, noting any modifications in their behavior caused by post-Ice Age environmental changes, by more recent cultural influences, and by anything they have learned since we met. And right away I spotted my first involuntary response. We all yawned.

Each of my animals began that first day of the new winter with a recognizable urge (Feeding Instinct), but as usual, while three dogs and an inside cat watched me closely, I ate first. Next, I fed the cat on the kitchen counter while again the dogs watched. The dogs and I then left the house to feed the outside cats. We were met at the door by the oldest female who displayed a notable example of acquired learning: Dogs do not chase cats who walk toward them. She was followed closely by the watch cat, our dominant male, whose morning instincts were in conflict (Feeding Instinct dislocated by Reproduction Instinct). Meanwhile, six young cats, last spring's kittens, hesitated near the cat enclosure, a conflict between two incompatible urges (Feeding Instinct versus Flight Instinct) until my collie sent them scrambling into the branches of a small tree. Joined by my younger Lhasa Apso, the collie barked and wagged his tail (a modification of the Aggression Instinct identified by Konrad Lorenz as Militant Enthusiasm.) I placed the cat food pan inside the enclosure where all eight cats took their places around it. Although at this point in our morning ritual only the cats and I had been satisfied, I had identified Lorenz's four basic instincts and come to another significant conclusion of my own: Dog does not eat dog — or cat.

My dogs and I then moved on to the corral gate where my two horses, a mare and her gelded colt, stood waiting for us. As usual, I went first to the gate to present two carrots, but because the morning was the coldest of the season I wore for the first time a heavy sheepskin coat with a high collar to protect my ears. As I approached the gate, the colt bolted. Horses are farsighted, an evolutionary adaptation developed when their ancestors moved from the woods to the open plain, discovering in the nick of evolutionary time that it was of greater survival value to recognize an enemy at a distance than a friend close by. In my new sheepskin coat the young horse did not know me and reacted predictably. (This is a variation of the Flight Instinct characterized by S. A. Barnett as Flight from Novelty.) At my greeting the colt returned to the gate to accept his carrot. We then moved to the stable where I served wafers of hay.

Pertinent to my morning's observations of animal behavior is this young horse's fear of hats. The horse's remarkable ability to learn what he is taught and to remember indefinitely what he has learned are two behavioral traits which have endeared his species to us. While these gifts are genetic, that is, up to him, what he learns in the service of man is cultural, that is, up to us. My young horse had a traumatic encounter with a cowboy early in his life. He identifies that awful moment with cowboy hats and will have nothing to do with anyone who wears one. When it rains I wear a modest beret. Also, all horses are torn between curiosity and suspicion, two of nature's conflicting preservatives, but because horses need glasses each of these instinctive responses is intensified. If evolutionary adaptation is still operative in horses, and there are those who believe it is not — Sir Julian Huxley has stated that the modern horse is stabilized — their vision must adjust its focus on the world in which both promise and threat have moved much closer.

Continuing our morning routine, two of the dogs and I set off on our morning walk, while the oldest, a Lhasa, took up her place at the driveway entrance to wait for us. This little dog, the smallest of my family, follows no pattern of behavior common to her species. She was born the runt in a litter of champions, too small to qualify for the show ring, too small, I was told, to be bred. She was sold at a bargain price because she was a remnant. Instead, she is a rare original. Given the chance to live, which in a wilder environment she would have been denied at birth, she became my daughter's companion, the bride of her male Lhasa and the mother of a perfect puppy. Her reaction to our rural world of larger animals and spaces was to ignore it and to create instead a world suited to her size and inclinations. She accepts the best chair, the front passenger seat of the car, the hollow behind my knees in bed as the natural order in a structured society where her superiority is deserved and worn with grace. Smaller than most cats, she simply walks through them. Unable to imagine a horse, she has never noticed them. She displays no evidence of acquired learning because she is the source of learning, the fountainhead from which the lessons of others originate. She is, of course, a dog, but she doesn't believe it.

The path we take each morning borders the pasture, an opportunity for the two other dogs to reestablish territorial markings at every clump of greasewood. My own markings, a five-strand barbed-wire fence, has long since been established, and while both borders may be functional, the dogs' perimeter is environmentally superior. The Territory Instinct has occupied biologists more than any other because it seems to demonstrate nature's solution to problems we have yet to solve. Its effect, of course, is to insure adequate food supply for each social or family group, to separate animals into compatible societies and to prevent overcrowding and starvation. Animals who inherit the Territory Instinct are supposed to live in civil harmony, to avoid murdering members of the same species and to shun imperialism. My dogs patrol a territory more than adequate for our needs, but again I noticed as we walked that both made regular sorties into neighboring territory, marking trees and flower beds not ours. I reminded them of this infringement, and they ran back wagging, but it seemed clear to me in my Darwinian role that they are impelled by an urge to colonize. Is the Territory Instinct offensive rather than defensive? Are we never satisfied?

It was still early on this morning of the winter solstice, and the rising sun and setting moon faced each other above opposite horizons. Frost had silvered the pasture, flocking the fence posts, stiffening the standing blades of rye grass, collecting like seed pearls along the grizzled spines of a small herd of steers and heifers. As the cattle saw us on the path they came to the fence, driven by deficiency in that frozen field, hoping for a handout from a bale of old hay outside the fence. The air around them was misted by their freezing breath and scented with the warm-milk smell I find so pleasant, but a small black heifer was missing from the tight-packed group. Then I saw her beyond the far fence. She had found an opening during the night, tested it for size and entered a neighbor's unfenced field in search of food. Now she stood outside the fence, as free as any cow would ever be, yet separated from the herd and therefore not free at all.

The Herd Instinct that impels the grazers to stay together is said to have little relationship to the family and community ties that bind more intelligent animals. Friendship and love have nothing to do with it, biologists say, and perhaps not. But my observations that morning of a small black heifer's anxiety, her wild dash across the pasture when she had been shown the way back, the relief she demonstrated as she squeezed between the warm flanks of her companions to grab a mouthful of frozen hay suggest a different conclusion. If the bonds of friendship are lacking among herd animals, perhaps our definition of the word and theirs do not agree.

What then are instincts? Are they involuntary responses, the antithesis of reason, as they have been defined, an evolutionary survival kit prepacked by the manufacturer with no instruction booklet? In fact, they often seem to inspire the most reasonable behavior. If not a part of acquired learning, how did they originate? Even by an evolutionary clock they could not always have been so diversified and so practical.

Are they still effective in a world where the top management has been taken over by a single species whose own behavior may be dangerously out of date? If not, can the responses we call instinctive be changed?

From our executive suite above the rest of the natural world we easily identify the behavior of those below us as unthinking, and the lower the species on our scale of intelligence, the more mindless we believe its behavior to be. We know that birds must learn to sing, but certainly not crickets. We know that men and women must study to become hydroengineers, but certainly not beavers. Yet, can the cooperation and experience necessary to build an air-conditioned castle on a tropic plain have been lodged in the first termite brain? If instinct guides the spider in the spinning of a perfect web, does it also prepare her to repair it after a heavy rain? Charles Darwin's *On The Origin of Species* has this to say: "An action, which we ourselves require experience to enable us to perform, when performed by an animal, more especially by a very young one, without experience, and when performed by many individuals in the same way, without their knowing for what purpose it is performed, is usually said to be instinctive. But I could show that none of these characters is universal. A little dose of judgment or reason . . . often comes into play, even with animals low in the scale of nature."

It is reasonable to assume that life began with the built-in urges to stay alive and to reproduce itself. It is also reasonable to assume that many of the ways each species has chosen to accomplish these vital objectives were accidental discoveries of a single innovator, adopted by entire populations because they worked. We now admit the influence of learning on biological behavior, reserving still the condition that where the lesson contradicts survival biology in time will cancel it. But it is also true that biology influences culture. Most of our own customs, laws and works of art derive from our emotions, our fears and our appetites. Evolutionary survival is the long record of lessons well learned, and to call each practical response instinctive because it has held true for a billion years or more is to belittle the teachers. Even those who believe that everyone but us is helplessly governed by a battery of genetic buttons pushed at the moment of creation admit that automatic response is subject to change by outside forces. Nothing has influenced animal behavior more, for instance, than the weather.

But response to ancient urges, lessons learned early and tested repeatedly over the eons, are not quickly replaced. Old reasons do not easily give way to new. The skunk still fears the silent owl more than the automobile; the turkey dreads the circling hawk, not Thanksgiving; and we still shrink from snakes and spiders, not guns and cigarettes.

Meanwhile, the complexity and the pace of change increase. Certainly, prehistoric patterns of behavior will no longer serve any but the most isolated and protected among us. And, paradoxically, it is those animals to whom mindlessness and subordinated individual choice are most apparent whose survival is least threatened. The communist ants will be here as long as there is oxygen, the doctrines of their patron unchanged and unchallenged, their genetic variation imperceptible.

The dogs and I headed for home. The collie led the way in a hip-swinging trot, the younger Lhasa at his heels, head down, tail up according to her breed. I brought up the rear, and ahead of us at the driveway entrance the smallest dog waited, a soft hump at the end of our path. When we joined her, she led us to the kitchen door, and we hurried after her. Her company at the end of our morning walk made it complete. I had listed all the separate instincts considered essential to my family's survival, noted considerable deviation in their application, and was left with the impression that each of us had behaved that morning according to the customs of our household, not the programmed impulses of our greatest grandfathers. Another thought also struck me.

Natural selection, Mr. Darwin's phrase for nature's way of assuring each species that only those best equipped to face the threat of extinction will live to reproduce themselves, is now being replaced by human selection, a subjective measurement of fitness. No longer does the world belong necessarily to the biggest and the strongest. According to the new rules, they may be the victims, while the small and the weak — and often the best — survive. If the behavior of the new selectors is unreasoning or out of date, then we are all in trouble. But if, as I must believe, instinctive behavior is rooted in reason and that however slowly, what is reasonable will prevail, what is unreasonable will be ultimately discarded, we may yet deserve our hegemony.

And a start has been made. My smallest dog was rejected by nature, selected by me. Survival for each of us has been served.

The Private Life of The Final Flower

In these days of growing concern for the survival of practically everything, I am optimistic about the dandelion. It is good to have something around that is not being investigated, threatened or diluted, whose integrity is intact, whose sex life is, if not happy, certainly assured, and whose only real enemy is a goose. The dandelion doesn't need worrying about.

In all of nature there is no organism which begins life with so magnificent an Emersonian leap into the air, which lives its first day with such irresponsibility, which sees so much of the world at no expense, yet which bogs down so deeply, resists change so fiercely as the dandelion. (Nothing, that is, except that last sentence.) The caterpillar, living its last day as a butterfly, may have something to look forward to, but the send-off a dandelion gets at an age to enjoy it is much more impressive. A dandelion has memories. A butterfly doesn't.

Joseph Wood Krutch, who called himself an amateur naturalist and who wrote more beautifully of nature than anyone I know of, believed that the dandelion would be the last survivor of our atomic age. This is partly because the dandelion is everywhere, but also because it is sexually self sufficient. Unlike most other plants, the dandelion does not need pollination to reproduce itself, and, therefore, being both male and female, the dandelion can get along without birds and bees and everybody else on earth.

But it is the dandelion's ability to get along so well with the rest of us that encourages me to be optimistic. Particularly, it is the California dandelion which seems to have solved the problem of the California gardner. Now that spring is here, the grass, heated by the sun, watered regularly by sprinklers, barbered by rotary mowers, is growing fast, and the dandelion is once again faced with its annual battle of wits. If it were to grow as other flowering plants do, lifting its blossoms proudly toward the sun to be noticed, it would be decapitated once a week. The California dandelion, however, needs to attract no one's attention, and so it huddles down below the level of the blade to blossom in safety. It lies low through the week, waiting until the Saturday gardener has pushed his power mower over it, never so much as nicking a petal. Then, moments after the danger is past, the dandelion hoists a tubular launcher above the grass. It is safe enough now to make its preparations for another generation of dandelions.

The gossamer balloon, riding atop the launcher, far enough above the ground for a clean takeoff, is the dandelion's final triumph. All it takes is an afternoon breeze and a hundred capsules sail away for a ride in the sky, each carefree, each containing within itself the wit and wisdom to survive wherever it falls. And somehow where it falls is usually another immaculate lawn.

Apparently, not all is gravy for the dandelion. I am told, although I have not verified it, that a single goose can uproot a yardful of dandelions. But this is no serious threat. Single geese are out of fashion these days, and double geese are more trouble than dandelions. There is also some concern being voiced by English scientists that the survival of the dandelion may be threatened by some insecticides.

But I remain optimistic. Any plant smart enough to hunker down under my mower, then rise up the moment I have passed to launch its seed in such a magnificent display of space-age bravado, any plant so well traveled, yet so much at home at my doorstep has little to fear. The dandelion's welfare is assured, not by social legislation, but by determined self sufficiency. Its freedom is secure because it relies on no one else to protect its rights. Its grace and beauty are the more enduring without an admiring glance.

Of course, there is always that single goose.

Peacocks!

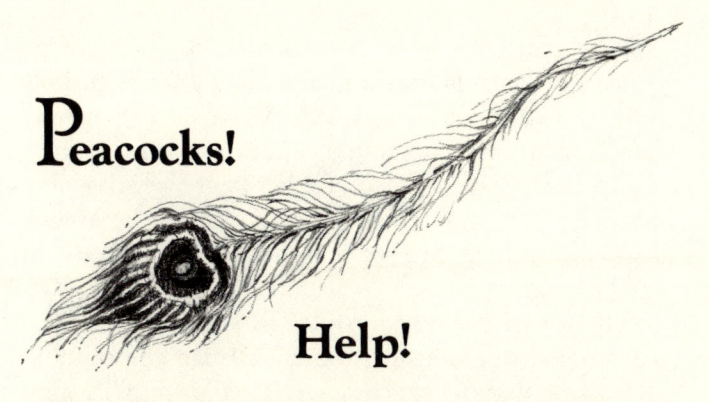

Help!

I have never been a bird watcher. I know they're up there. They know I'm down here. That's the way we like it. But lately a bird has been watching me and making me nervous. Not only is he almost as big as I am, tail included, but he insists that I watch him too. If I hide, he comes looking for me, peeking at me through the windows, posing like Petrouchka. When that fails, he walks on my roof where he sounds as if he were wearing golf shoes. Of course, he isn't. Only big spiked feet. When I hear him up there I sneak out under the eaves where I wait, hose at the ready, nozzle turned to needle spray until he peeks over the edge of the roof. Then ZAP! I soak his tail. He hates that. He runs home until his tail dries out. But there are more where he came from. I may be the only man in America whose right of privacy has been invaded by a bunch of abusive peacocks.

I owe this intolerable intrusion to my next-door neighbor, a woman I have always admired because she leaves me alone except when I need her. She has been a perfect neighbor, sensible and country practical until in a moment of madness she bought three peafowl. She was never one to indulge in the foolishness the rest of us find irresistible the moment we escape from leash laws. She keeps geese for family reunions. She keeps a dog to guard the geese, except that he didn't. One hungry cat patrols her barn, and her garden is entirely edible. And she loves to weed. When she gets behind her Roto-tiller she weeds my yard too. When I protest, softly, she tells me it is good for her figure, which is very good. Yet, this noble woman paid cash for a peacock and two peahens and set them loose to peck away at my privacy.

There was nothing I could do about it. Country neighbors live according to the Christian admonition: "He that is without sin among you, let him cast the first stone." My veterinarian built his boarding kennels next to a pig farm, assuming correctly that odor would cancel bark. My youngest dog brings home shredded socks from my neighbor's clothesline every wash day. To have complained about her peacocks would have been to violate the truce we live by. And also, at first I was impressed.

I saw my first up-close peacock posing one morning like a huge hood ornament on the front of my truck, and, like all who first come upon this incredible bird, I stared. That was what I was supposed to do. His crested head jerked from side to side so that I could admire it, his electric-blue neck rolled with his head spasms, and the rest of him stretched like a feather boa above thin white legs. His folded wings were the color of English tweed, his waistcoat was russet, and his tail, folded on this occasion, was emerald green. The costume was eye watering. Later, he brought the peahens over to visit. They were less gaudy, but no turkeys either. Crested like the cock, necks to match his tail, they wore more subdued earth colors on their plump bodies. Together they strutted over to inspect the private park. Peacocks on my terrace! For a moment I felt like Solomon himself.

Early one afternoon when my dogs and I were napping, the peafowl trio returned. My Lhasas saw them first from the window bench where they lie to guard my castle. As the birds approached across the lawn, my dogs, true to their Tibetan ancestry, ran through an open door to meet them. Faced with two loud little dogs, the peahens took off, heading for my roof. The peacock, dragging his train, tried to follow but failed to gain sufficient altitude. Instead, he crashed through my bedroom window, sending glass shards flying across my bed and landing in a tangle of loose feathers on the window bench. We lay there, he and I, staring at each other, both in shock, both forever afterward at war.

I called my neighbor. She rushed to my bedroom where she bundled the peacock under her arm like a week's laundry and disappeared. In minutes she was back with the good news that the bird was unhurt. She then lifted the window out of its frame and disappeared again, promising to return. Within an hour she carried in a new window, lifted it into place, and panted an apology. "I always thought they could fly better than that," she said. She sounded disappointed.

And so the peacock war began. It is a contest I know I can't win, nor is there any possibility of safe retreat. My only defense is exposure, to warn all who might otherwise be tempted to live too close to peacocks. The truth has never been fully revealed. A trip to the library confirmed that peacock literature is deceptive, awash in awe and admiration. Prized by kings since Solomon because it is uncommon, immortalized by the insecure because it most definitely is not, the peacock has bluffed its way through history. Alexander The Great was taken in. William Blake called its pride "the glory of God," and even Darwin admired the bird, although apparently from a distance. The Vikings stuck peacock feathers in their hats. India proclaimed the peacock its national bird. Only Aristotle saw the peacock for what it is, a pest. He noted that peacocks threw roof tiles at him, and I don't doubt it for a moment.

This is not to say that peacocks have nothing going for them. They are odorless and can wiggle their ears, for instance, but their pride, that flimsy fan above the tail, turns out on closer inspection to have been a disaster. Those spreading plumes, dotted with giant's eyes, are supposed to turn peahens into blushing brides, but instead the peahens don't even turn around. Each time the peacock unfurls his rickety pride with the crackling sound of a fat man sinking into a rattan chair, pivots for applause and expects the girls to come running, the peahens ignore him. As they continue their pecking progress, the plumes wilt and the peacock hurries after them, dragging his pride like a used parachute. A peacock in full plume is also helpless in a stiff breeze, I am pleased to report, and grounded when his pride is wet. At summer's end the fan is a bundle of sticks which drop off, leaving the peacock with nothing more to wave than an old brown stump. For some reason, however, dogs enjoy chewing peacock plumes, so the pride of the peacock is not entirely wasted.

In my second year of the peacocks, and in spite of his foolish performance, my neighbor's peacock produced six duplicates. Nine peafowl patrolled my yard, scattering cats, stabbing at every blossom, trampling window boxes. They perched in my trees, strolled on my roof, and spattered my terrace. Peeping, prying, posturing they came, these pompous parasites, their self esteem protected by thousands of years of pampering. I chased them, shouted, beat kitchen pans together, but it was hopeless. They ran off only to return. One dissenter every four thousand years cannot dent a peacock's pride.

Much has been written about the peacock's cry, but

nowhere near enough. Surrounded, I have devoted sleepless nights to a study of their raucous language. Peacocks, it is said, can be heard two miles away, but I listen at much closer range and have separated their vocabulary into four responses, all bad. Although by day the birds are by no means silent, the moment they become invisible they go mad. Their first night sound is a repeated demand, HELP! It is not a distress signal, of course, but, like the bird itself, a false alarm. Robbed of admiration, the peacock screams his plea. HEELLLPP! The unanswered cry grows more demanding, the single syllable stretched and falling in pitch.

The second peacock sound, uttered always after the first has failed, is a muttered expletive, the unprintable phrase a sailor's parrot might use. It is all but impossible to ignore. Time after time I have caught myself answering in kind, adding only the word TOO! I am not certain that peahens also use this foul language, and I like to think they don't. It is the sulking response of a sore loser and not at all feminine.

The third and fourth peacock noises are also sequential and revealing. Because the bird has crossed the world for centuries at the deliberate pace of one who must be noticed, his strut must not be hurried. Each step is artfully synchronized by a system of peacock pullies connecting legs and neck. If the peacock is forced to run he goes to pieces and becomes just another chicken, his charm-school carriage abandoned. On these occasions he clucks and squawks like any barnyard bird. At a safe distance, he gives the final blast, a fearful HONK closer in pitch and intensity to the horn of a diesel locomotive than to the sound of a goose. Again, it is the cry of the punctured ego, the empty threat of the discredited fraud.

One fact which justifies the peacock's sense of security is that he is virtually inedible. He was born to be seen and certainly to be heard, but not to be eaten. He can run, but not fast enough, yet few predators, including man, have bothered to catch him. Throughout history the peacock has been eaten only by the gluttonous and the starving. The Romans, who were willing to try anything, served peacock tongues and peacock brains, but without calls for seconds. Peacock tongues, like their language, are tough. Peacock brains, long unused, are flaccid. Again, in the Middle Ages an effort was made to swallow the peacock. Roast peacock and peacock pie were served at medieval feasts, and every culinary trick was used to make the bird look appetizing. Roast peacock with plumes rising from the platter and encircled with prunes, which had recently been discovered and were all the rage, still could not compare with roasts of pheasant, goose and duck. In France knights took the Vow of The Peacock, a pledge of valor whose first test presumably was to swallow a bit of the bird.

Concensus has it that peacock tastes like tough chicken and should be shunned if there is any choice at all. My own observations reinforce this conclusion. One morning last winter when floods and frosts had all but eliminated food sources for wildlife I came upon great puddles of white feathers in my pasture. Coyotes, never known to venture into our fenced and cross-fenced society, had been driven from the hills to my neighbor's yard. There they were presented with a choice of entrees, goose or peacock. Not one peacock was missing.

The peacock will never become an endangered species. He will fade away instead like an old vaudevillian after the applause has died. Estimates of his lifespan range between ten and thirty-five years, a discouraging statistic, but I am resigned. With the unerring instinct the unwelcome have for barging in where they are not wanted the peacock will migrate to my yard, there to mock me by day and curse me by night. As darkness blurs his colors the air will fill with helpless cries like those of guests trapped in a burning hotel. My roof will remain a peacock walk, my yard a peacock park, and only now and then will the thrill of counterattack be mine.

In May a peahen settled into a hay bale in my barn to sit out spring on who knows how many eggs. (I am told they often lay six or eight.) I came upon her when I tried to clean out last year's hay before the new crop is stored. We faced each other, that peahen and I, our relationship for the first time reversed. Now she wanted privacy, and I was the prying intruder.

"See what it's like?" I asked her.

She looked away for a moment, then met my stare. She knew she was safe, and so did I. A man also has his pride.

The Starling Rodeo

In my country September is really two months. Its place at the end of summer makes it a time for celebrating the partnership of sun and earth, the gathering of their gifts. Its place at the edge of winter makes September a time to prepare, tempering festivity with warning. The September mind sharpens with the air, conscious of the shortening days, alert to their significance in the longer cycle of our lives. There is April in early morning. The afternoon breeze comes from August, but its targets, the leaves and grasses, rattle with despair. Evening penetrates. Night overwhelms. We celebrate September victories as we prepare to win them. We are ahead at the seventh-inning stretch.

Like the fenceposts at my pasture line, September divides sun and shadow, but the shadow deepens and there is uneasiness at noon. The eyes of all who look to me for winter solutions are upon me now. The false springs I have created with my summer fountains no longer tempt the grasses. They have tasted fall. The urgent need to prepare brings strange supplicants to my door. A hummingbird, who needs ten times my energy to survive, pays daily visits to my flower pots, but as he moves from crinkled petunia to seedy snapdragon, pausing and rejecting, his tsks of disapproval are loud.

He has often expressed his disgust with my garden, banking off to better places, but now there is no time to waste. His time is short. I want to call, "I tried, I tried," but you can't make excuses to a hummingbird.

Someone has done better at my kitchen counter. There I keep a loaf of homemade bread. (How a man who lives alone and without the talent to bake bread comes by a homemade loaf is my secret.) On a recent morning the bread had been removed from its plastic bag and nibbled end to end. A soft and silent sandwich maker had walked into my kitchen while we slept. The risk was worth it.

In September I hear the breakfast call from the corral. Since early spring my horses have taken breakfast where it grows, but now it must be served. The mare and her son have chosen Prince, our ancient gelding, to sound the breakfast call on the aluminum Lifetime Gate because only Prince wears shoes. He is working now on his third Lifetime Gate, having stamped two others into twisted scrap. The manufacturer of Lifetime Gates does not specify whose lifetime he had in mind. Obviously, it is not Prince's. I respond to the call. Later in the day I hear the bird machine singing in the vineyard half a mile to the west. It is an unpleasant sound and intended to be because the bird machine is an electronic scarecrow, an amplified scissoring which goes off once every five minutes while the sun is up to keep birds from the ripening grapes. It sounds somewhat like a bluejay's strident cry, but it can be heard clearly for half a mile.

Celebration is in order. Mine is a rodeo renewed each morning as the sun finds the pasture. A flock of starlings settles in three close-packed rows along a section of the three-rail fence. They sit wing to wing, chattering their excitement, placing small bets. Before them in the grass are six fat heifers, five mixed Angus and

Hereford, one the color of vanilla ice cream. At a secret signal five starling cowboys fly to the back of the vanilla heifer. There these daredevils ride until the last one is shaken off. Five more volunteers from the audience take their places then as excitement grows along the fence rails. Feet shift, wings refold. Only when I come too close does the rodeo end and the audience leave in formation.

Why do starling cowboys choose to ride a vanilla-ice-cream cow? Why not a black one? I have decided it is because starlings are also hams. If you are going to show off, you have to be seen.

September ends ominously under low clouds and fog, clearing just soon enough to gather into offshore bundles for a midnight return. Once again we become conscious of the sky, the chill at evening. Celebration is over. Preparations begin. September ends by isolating us as winter does. We are on our own, but never quite. Across the fog bank a hoof clatters on the Lifetime Gate. The S. S. Prince has docked.

The Fur That Flies

Recently, a Pentagon correspondent for Reuter's reported that a synthetic substitute for bat guano had been found. CBS and NBC News announced that bat guano, previously imported from Canadian bat caves, is an essential product used by the U. S. Army. A CBS reporter added that holders of stock in Canadian bat caves might consider selling.

It is, perhaps, understandable that any population of mammals which exceeds the earth's human population by more than three to one would be considered alarming and possibly dangerous. We hate to be outnumbered. It is less obvious, however, why so little is known about bats, or, for that matter, why any animal weighing half an ounce or less should frighten so many much larger people. Few of us have ever seen a bat. They prefer to fly after sunset and are not easily seen even by owls who keep the same hours and are out looking for them, and the great majority of bats does not live in the temperate zones of the earth. Even fewer of us know bat fact from fiction. Bats, for instance, do not like long hair, nor do they make other entangling alliances except among themselves. Few animals are more fragile or more exclusive. Nor is it true that bats bite people unless given no choice. They devote more time to cleaning themselves than we do, carry fewer parasites than dogs and cats, and, according to Dr. Alvin Novick, who with photographer Nina Leen has written *The World of Bats*, a book which would have become a bat lover's bible if there were any bat lovers, only a single instance of human rabies definitely attributed to a bat's bite had been recorded in U. S. medical files by 1969.

Why, then, have bats remained totally disliked? Why do people who say they like all animals hate bats? And what is the U. S. Army doing with bat guano, real or synthetic? Difficult as it may be to drop a few clichés from the language, painful as it may be to change our minds, we must do so. In an overcrowded world, limited in resources unequally shared, only the complete understanding of all creatures and their true relationship to man may save us. Let's begin with ten billion bats.

Bats make poor first impressions because many of them have funny faces. Among the more than twelve hundred identified species are such small hobgobblins as the Greater Mustache Bat, the Dog-faced Bat, the Spear-nosed Bat, the Leaf-nosed Bat, the Bulldog Bat, the Short-nosed Bat, the Hoary and Horseshoe Bats, and even the Slit-faced Bat. There are hundreds of bats with perfectly normal faces, but we seldom see pictures of these. Instead, we stare at squashed little faces with pugnacious noses and bug eyes, distorted as the faces of children flattened agains the outside of a candy-store window. Bat faces have been fashioned for every practical purpose, usually associated with their remarkable ability to receive and interpret sounds in order to zero in on unseen targets and to avoid bumping into obstacles which might do real damage to their profiles. Why some bats can handle their complex systems of accoustical orientation without rabbit ears or cauliflower noses, while others cannot, is one of the many questions about bats still unanswered. The fact remains that most of the bats commonly photographed have faces only another bat would love.

Also, any bat on the wing is hard for us to believe because nothing else with fur flies. (Flying squirrels do not fly; using winglike flaps stretching from front to hind feet, they glide, and always downward.) That the bat, who is an animal with obviously no business up in the air on wings which appear flimsy and homemade, should still be up there is unnatural and therefore sinister. We have tried to do it, so we know it cannot be done.

Nor are bats blind. All have eyes of various sizes (each eye is of course always the same size on the same bat), but there are bat experts who predict that bats will in time lose their eyesight because they do not need to navigate by sight nor to see their prey. But, like those marine biologists who say whales do not need noses and will ultimately lose them, forecasters of bat evolution with better hind- than foresight could find better ways to spend their time. "Blind as a bat" is just more bat balderdash, and bats do need eyes for at least one essential purpose: to differentiate between day and night. Also, bat knees and elbows bend the wrong way, which makes them suspicious. They have feet, but they rarely walk. Instead, they drag their hind feet through the air, using them in somewhat the way airplanes use wing flaps to steer and to land.

The most off-putting physical equipment of bats are, of course, their leathery wings which span a triangular space between outstretched fingers and ankles. Their wings, proportionately larger and with greater lift than birds' wings, which, being made of feathers, leak, enable bats to maneuvre in midair and to take off faster than most birds can. A bat with a hole in his wing has had it.

Paradoxically, resentment against bats may also be rooted in the subconcious awareness of the real possibility that we and they share common prehistoric ancestors. Bats are believed to belong to the primate family, as do apes and men. Their thumbs are opposable, as only the thumbs of primates are. Most bats, like people, produce a single offspring at a time. Twins and triplets are rare. Furthermore, bats seem to die of old age absolutely worn out from the efforts of a long life. This may be one reason the Chinese have made the bat a symbol of long life and happiness, but, next to bats, the Chinese are the most enigmatic of mammals. Bats also enjoy planned parenthood, although who the planners were is not known. A male bat may deposit his sperm in the female in the fall of the year when he is feeling exceptionally frisky, but the normal pregnancy cycle is postponed so that the female gives birth not during the winter when she is weak or asleep, but in the spring when food is again plentiful. How about that?

The most important reason for the seemingly hopeless gap between us and bats is their lifestyle. Most bats spend eighty percent of their lives hanging upside down by their opposable thumbs. We cannot imagine it. Nor can we see ourselves gathered in bunches on the roofs of caves, which bats prefer to belfries ad attics wherever there is a choice. And, although bats have sound reasons for flying at night, we seldom consider them. Bats choose darkness both because their principal source of food, insects, are also out then and because most of their enemies are unable to see them. Bats aren't dumb. Nevertheless, Aesop, who leaped to more than one questionable conclusion, wrote: "He that is neither one thing nor the other has no friends."

The built-in sonar of bats is their most remarkable feature. Bats are able to emit sounds either through nose or mouth which cover a wide frequency range, some audible to the human ear, others supersonic beeps. They employ frequency modulation, harmonics, octave leaps and sophisticated dynamics to adjust their echolocation equipment to determine the size and nature of their target, its speed and direction, and its altitude relative to them. By this combination of audio-visual awareness they regulate their own flight patterns so that their signals will not alert a predator but will bounce off a moth. Bats also cary some sort of ear plug so that only a returning squeak can be heard. This may keep bats from being confused, but its operation has confused people who have tried to figure it out.

Bats, like other hibernating animals, also have temperature controls and seem to be highly sensitive to climatic change. Bats common in the northern parts of the United States fly to Georgia and Alabama for the winter, although no one has yet figured out how they know which way is south. Others hibernate and can remain barely alive with a body temperature in the low 40's during the cold months. Southern bats avoid intense heat by living in moist, sunless caves. Some tropical bats are fruit eaters, others fish eaters, but most are insectivorous, consuming up to half their body weight each night. Thousands of tons of bugs are caught and eaten each year by bats, including many we hate worse than we hate bats, yet bats go thankless.

Then there are the vampire bats, inhabitants of Central and South America, whose food is the blood of larger animals. Vampire bats do not suck the blood; they pierce the skin and lap the trickle as it flows from cattle and other grazers. Again, vampire bats have been dealt with unfairly, not only because they do not attack people, but because they were named by early European biologists, many of whom spent the nineteenth century sailing around the world naming whatever they saw. Vampires of the Count Dracula variety are the inventions of European horror-story writers, and vampire bats, who never lived in Europe, simply got stuck with the name.

Still, people with bats in their houses want to evict them. In areas of the world where bats are most numerous, batproof architecture is replacing structures once thick with bats. In this country, however, where bats are not often household guests, no foolproof bat remedy has been devised. I consulted my local Animal Control Officer for his suggestions and was told that the best remedy is "exclusion," that is, keeping bats out in the first place by placing wire mesh across all possible bat entrances. That kind of common sense is what makes great Animal Control Officers. He also added that hanging bags of camphor crystals in attics and leaving electric lights burning in attics have sometimes proved effective. "But there is really no way to dislodge bats," he added helpfully.

A neighbor of mine has lived in the same house since it was built sixty years ago. She confessed to me that she loves all animals except bats, filling bird feeders, leaving food outside her door for every wild creature. Yet, as long as she can remember there has been a colony of bats living in the unused attic of her house, waiting, perhaps, for her to like them too.

Which brings us to the publicity bats received from the press. Bats are homebodies fond of communal living, and they produce quantities of guano on the floors of caves where ten thousand to ten million bats may live out their lives in a single cavern in parts of southern United States and Mexico. Visitors to bat caves have described the atmosphere as rather close, but the buildup of guano in such places has brought high profits to men with no serious objection from the bats. Bat guano is rich in nitrates and has long been marketed as expensive fertilizer.

But its use by the army still puzzled me. Not confident that I would be enlightened, I called the Pentagon and was eventually routed to Lt. Colonel Wade in the Office of Information Services, a jovial voice from Washington and a man familiar with the Reuter's bat story. "It all started," he explained, "because the army uses a chemical compound called nitroguanadine as a propellant in firing artillery and tank ammunition. Nitroguanadine produces less wear on gun bores and longer range.

"But nitroguanadine doesn't come from bat manure," Colonel Wade assured me. "We import a chemical from Canada called guanine which, when combined with sulphuric acid becomes nitroguanadine and is then shipped to our ordinance facility in Sunflower, Kansas. The Reuter's man simply invented the bat guano connection and fooled everybody. We all had a good laugh."

Colonel Wade and I laughed, but briefly at coast-to-coast telephone rates, and said goodbye. At first, I felt disappointed. One more piece of bat fiction. Then I began to feel happy that bats were not participating in the small wars taking place in Sunflower, Kansas. They have been blamed for almost everything else. On further reflection, Colonel Wade's easy answers began to bother me. Pentagon spokesmen have a way with fiction themselves, so I checked Webster's to learn that guanine is a crystalline substance "used in the production of nitroguanadine, especially found in the guano of birds and certain animals." Still, the Canadian connection made little sense. Bat guano is found in quantities sufficient even for the army in bat caves where bats live the year round, caves located in warm and tropical climates. The only bats found in Canada are the Big-eared Bat and the Little Brown Bat, common also in New England. But these bats are not found in large numbers in Canada, and those who are there either go south for the winter or hibernate. It seemed unlikely that Canadian bats would produce enough guano to satisfy the Pentagon, and Texas, which I believe is still within its jurisdiction, has long been a source of bat guano.

I am not privy to Pentagon secrets, let alone Pentagon logic, so I am unable to dispute Colonel Wade's explanation of the story. Common bat sense tells me, however, that if the army is using bat guano in the form of guanine for its purposes, they have not told Colonel Wade about it and they are not importing it from Canada. I am grateful to the Reuter's wag who made up the story, however, for it inspired me to learn more about bats and to think kindly of them.

Did you know, for instance, that mother bats come equipped with false nipples which serve as handles for their babies to hold on to during the mother bat's hair-raising night flights?

Now who but a bat would have thought of that?

The Fourth Cat

Once again a member of my family whose first days I remember well is living out her last beside me. I was not that much younger when my daughter brought home a gray-striped kitten in her arms to announce breathlessly that another little girl in her class was selling gray-striped kittens "for free" and that she had bought one. She named the kitten Liki, short for Little Kitten, and that was what she was only fifteen years ago.

We are all older now, of course, and the years have changed us. My daughter is twenty-three, a young lady, and I well, I was always the oldest. But Liki was never old. She soon turned into a rather portly cat whose pale yellow eyes became hot pools of luminescent greens when she met my headlights late at night. Almost from the beginning she displayed an even temper. She made her way through dogs and children with unruffled dignity. She washed both sides of her face with her left paw, and when I scratched the spot at the base of her spine she couldn't reach herself she lifted her face in ecstasy and stuck out her tongue.

Long ago she lost a canine which gave her a lopsided yawn, but the missing tooth offered small comfort to the gophers in her path, or the rare wrong-headed mouse foolish enough to nest in her kitchen.

Nor does she show her centenary years. Only the other morning on her way to the sycamore she uses as a ladder to the roof where she takes the sun until late afternoon she chased a falling leaf, flipping it along before her, then waving it away when the breeze abandoned it. Later that day she joined the dogs and me to walk to the end of the road before signaling with a silent cry her readiness to be carried on my shoulder the rest of the way. She could have walked, but riding there, her velvet flank against my ear, I hear her purr her satisfaction that I have not forgotten her special place in my life.

The first indication that something inside my cat was wearing out came a few weeks ago when none of the usual dinner choices I offer tempted her. It has been nearly ten years since she became my cat, inherited with two small dogs from grownup children, and I know her eating habits. At first, I bought the most expensive choices from the cat can shelves only to discover that she preferred the least expensive chicken and tuna combination, a most uncatlike fancy. Of course, I offered tastes from any meal of mine which included turkey or chicken or fish, and I learned quickly that only when she heard the sound of the electric can opener, proof that her dinner would be fresh and new, would she eat at all. Leftovers chilled in the refrigerator were never fit for her. Then the morning came when none of her favorites suited her. That night I stewed a chicken just for her.

Even while she nibbled selectively from her dish I knew what I didn't want to know, that again in my lifetime another life still new to me was about to end.

And I reflected bitterly upon the injustice of nature's unfortunate equation: that my life is measured by five cat lives and that once more it was about to be disconnected. Among symbiotic species, those whose differences complement and sustain each other, the choice cats and dogs and we have made to accompany each other throughout our lives is surely the most rewarding. That the lifetimes we share should be so uneven seems to contradict an evolutionary decree.

Although my cat continued to appear at mealtimes, announcing her appetite by crossing and recrossing my shins, her indifference to her usual fare increased, and somehow I must be to blame. I roamed the aisles of the market in search of delicacies I had never bought before. I brought home cans of baby shrimp and minced clams and Dungeness crabmeat. Startled by such a variety of tastes, she tried them all and withdrew to polish her whiskers with enough to revitalize her. And I began to enjoy her leftovers. For the first time since I have been preparing my own meals my dinners began with hors d'oeuvres, smoked salmon and an occasional paté. I discovered boneless turkeys and Cornish game hens, and because for her each gourmet delight lost its savor if repeated I began to gain pounds while she lost precious ounces. Still, through the early weeks of autumn she went on with life as usual, moving with the sun across the roof, grooming herself carefully before descending heavily from the sycamore in the late afternoons to the waiting smorgasbord.

The morning came in mid-October when my cat would not bring herself to taste any of my suggestions. It was the day I had been postponing, the day to take her to the veterinary clinic for tests which would identify the reason for her failing appetite. Before the blood sample was drawn from a shaved foreleg, however, I knew that I was bringing in another patient who by that accepted ratio of cat years to human years had outlived her time. While she stood between us on the examining table, sleek and alert and unaware that she had violated an actuarial computation assigning her the years already behind her, the diagnosis would be all too clear. My cat was just too old. What more could I expect than fifteen years? We were lucky, she and I. We had stolen time and gotten away with it.

When the veterinarian called me the next afternoon with the laboratory results, failing liver and kidneys, he reminded me again that cats and men are mortal. Dialysis by machine was not practical for cats and what cat would choose to live that way? Rather, he told me, enjoy her last weeks and spare her pain. That was exactly what I intended to do, had always done, but this time I would do more. I would introduce my cat to a better life than even a well-attended family cat had ever known. Not only would our daily meetings be heralded with extra flourishes, small courtesies and considerations, she and I would continue to defy the timekeepers. We would steal more time and use it well.

A priority in our cat hospice, of course, became my efforts to persuade her by whatever guile to eat. She must discover the difference between swallowing a few bites each day and *dining*. When I am alone I prefer to sit in a director's chair at an open bar between the kitchen and the family room, facing the evening television news and well above the circle of dogs waiting patiently for handouts. My cat also likes this canvas-seated perch, but at mealtimes I displace her. Now she would displace me. That evening I put her in the director's chair, then pulled up a stool to sit beside her. I had cooked chicken in white wine to celebrate her new life and I passed her small pieces one at a time from my plate. Perhaps it was her favorite chair, or it could have been the wine, but she ate every bite I handed to her. Below us the four dogs watched in silent wonder, but later while she washed her face I handed down the last scraps to the audience.

My cat and I continued to dine *a deux*, she in the director's chair, our pace slowed to permit rumination. She was willing to return to her old favorites, the cheapest cat cans, providing that we sat together and that I allowed her time to reconsider. Every few days I prepared fowl cooked slowly in a mild chablis with, perhaps, a dash of basil for piquancy. She enjoyed surprise, especially an unexpected herb in a savory sauce. Her willingness to extend this coda of her life depended upon the ingenuity of the chef, and because she could not take more than a few bites at a sitting I made each bite an adventure.

The objective of our mealtime ritual of tantalizing tastes was to prolong my cat's life, but I also wanted her to enjoy living as never before. This presented me with a far greater challenge because I have always believed that cats know more of the joys of living than any other creature except, possibly, otters. Unlike us, cats never outgrow their delight in cat capacities, nor do they settle finally for limitations. Cats, I think, live out their lives fulfilling their expectations. One of their supreme accomplishments is their successful blending of solitude and society. In a family of cats, such as the seven who live outside my door, there is a benign estrangement understood by all. They meet affectionately at the dinner pan like neighbors at a potluck supper, enjoying togetherness because it is temporary, scattering to private niches afterward to enjoy their own company. It would not do to force my attentions upon my cat or to presume that I knew a better way to spend her extra days than she.

Then, too, there was the fateful gap that separated us; I alone knew her days were numbered. It should follow that I knew better how to make them count, but did I? Had I made more of the four cats lives behind me than she had of her one? And then I realized that my ministrations were intended as much for my sake as for hers, that when she ate I felt replenished, that it was I who welcomed each extra day we enjoyed for what it was, a gift. It was not I who was teaching my cat to gather rosebuds, but she who was teaching me. Nevertheless, there were expressions of love and concern for her I must add to our relationship, whatever the reasons. I noticed that she was finding it more difficult to come down from her climbing tree than to climb it. She seemed to find landing on hard ground painful, so I began to watch for her appearance on the limb leading to the roof, and when I saw her hesitating there I went to the base of the tree and lifted her down. She accepted this small service and waited for me to help her.

My efforts to extend and to enrich my cat's last days received support from an unexpected ally. October, normally a month of abrupt change from lingering Indian summer days to first frosts and the chilling fringes of Arctic storms lapping their way southward, stood still. Throughout the month the skies remained clear, the sun warm. They were days made to the order of an old cat. Only the nights warned of hard times ahead for the frail. The weeks of smaller portions, often interrupted by days when she could hold no food at all, had taken their toll, apparent in the deepening hollows along her flanks and the emerging points of hips and shoulders. I decided that she needed an auxiliary heating unit, me.

Although my family includes four dogs and my bed is large, for good reasons I have always limited my sleeping companions to the two oldest and smallest dogs. I learned long ago that two dogs never sleep on the same side of me and that each must have a hollow created by my sleeping on my side in a horizontal crouch. As the nights grow colder and the thermostat of the electric blanket is turned higher, my dogs on the outside of the blanket press closer until I am tightly wrapped in place. Turning over is not worth the sighs it causes.

When I decided to add my cat to this long-established positioning two problems were created. Cats prefer not only sleeping hollows but hollows protected on all sides. And no cat, even mine, is willing to share her nest with a dog who snores. I would have to provide a third hollow, one which would give her a private place between the dogs. After a night of practice I found that by assuming a position similar to that of a sprinter at the start of a race, right leg stretched and slightly bent at the knee, left leg tucked high so that it formed two sides of an isosceles triangle as my left foot rested against my right shin, I could create a third hollow while preserving the other two. Moreover, I could maintain this position quite comfortably.

I was ready to introduce my cat to her new bed. I waited until both dogs were settled and the light out, then carried her to bed and assumed my horizontal sprinter's pose and pushed her into the three-sided hollow. She sat there for several minutes, then shook herself and returned to her kitchen shelf, obviously leery of the mosaic I had created for her. The next night, a particularly cold one, I let her take the initiative, and as soon as the light was out I felt her arrive on my stomach. Quickly I froze into position as she walked down into her hollow. As she lay against my leg I felt her shivering. Then, as she settled deeper into the warm blanket the trembling stopped and when I reached down to place a reassuring hand on her I heard the steady purr she saves for me.

It is November now and my cat is noticeably weaker, but still enjoying our days. I watch her carefully, alert for the first sign of pain. I must not waiver when discomfort becomes unbearable, but we will know, she and I, and I'll stay with her while she goes to sleep. Afterwards a sympathetic friend will ask, "Why do you put yourself through it?" For fifteen years of the pleasure of her company, that's why. Grief is the obverse of happiness. They are two sides of a single coin, and only the vulnerable know either.

Another cat? Perhaps. For love there is also a season; its seeds must be resown. But a family cat is not replaceable like a wornout coat or a set of tires. Each new kitten becomes its own cat and none is repeated. I am four cats old, and since it is necessary to exchange friends, perhaps.

But it is still too soon to think about another cat. It is nearly dark outside and the roof is cold. My cat will be making her way along the sycamore limb and I must be there waiting to lift her to my shoulder. Today I found fresh swordfish in the market, $5.45 a pound, and she has never tasted swordfish. Maybe she'll be tempted.

If not, she'll sit a while on my lap in our director's chair and I will feel the sun she carries in her coat.

The Lake That Burps

Tucked into a craggy nest formed by the peaks of half a dozen stragglers from the San Rafael range in the northwest corner of the Santa Ynez Valley in Santa Barbara County, California, is a puddle of fathomless water as round as a giant's eye. In a wetter part of the world it would be called a pond, but here where a dry rock bed is a creek and a river is only a river now and then, water is exaggerated, and this dark jewel is called Zaca Lake.

Although the crests that protect it, like the huddled heads of old men, some bald except for a fringe of wild oat grass creamy white in summer, others sparsely covered with half-starved pines and scrub brush, appear to have once formed the muzzle of an ancient volcano, the walls of Zaca are believed to have been created by earth slippage. No gem could find a more flattering setting. And because the bottom at its center has never been touched, Zaca has been called bottomless for a century. Its name, variously translated, is probably a

Chumash Indian word spelled to resemble the Spanish word *saca*, or sack, and is thought to mean "hidden waters" or "quiet place." Nothing about Zaca, however, is very definite. Least understood is its behavior, for Zaca Lake has a digestion problem which causes it to burp at least twice a year.

Zaca has survived, not only as the last natural lake in the county, but just as it was before man arrived at its shores. One reason is its inaccessibility. A century ago it was half a day's journey from the nearest settlement by horse and buggy over a winding path which plunges into dells of live oak, then rises by hairpin turns to one of the mountain peaks. Even today the trip to Zaca is only for the determined. Seven miles over the rubble left by winter runoff, seven miles of pursuing dust and popping boulders lie between the nearest modern road and the prehistoric shoreline. Then, even to the mildest Thorovian, the comparison to Henry's pond is compelling. Like Walden, "it is a clear and deep green well," whose evening surface is a watercolor painted from both sides, cracked momentarily by the gasp of a catfish, shattered by the plowing feet of a settling duck, otherwise a mirror as changeable as "watered silks and sword blades." Like Walden, Zaca has no inlet and no outlet. It is replenished by inner springs flowing from crevices no man has seen. Like Walden its shores are fringed by foliage as delicate as the curling lashes around an eye.

Unlike the Massachusetts pond, Zaca Lake is a mere thirty-five acres, whereas Thoreau claimed sixty-one and a half for Walden. And, while during Thoreau's stay he could see clearly to the sandy bottom, Zaca's depths are impenetrable. Falling away immediately to a depth of twenty feet or more, the lake waters darken into a watery night, deepening even the reflected blue of a noon sky. Nor are the fish that populate Zaca the perch and pickerel of Walden Pond. Rather, they are catfish clouds moving just beneath the surface, as if nervously anticipating trouble from below. And they will not be disappointed, for the digestive system of the lake has long since proven too much for bass and bluegill caught in one of its periodic upheavals.

Nor is it likely that the fish in Zaca share a taste for music. Thoreau charmed the perch in his pond with the sound of his flute, but Zaca fish have been a captive audience for concerts calculated to unsettle even a well adjusted fish. One of the many owners of the lake, a Frenchman named Libeu, was so fond of his native anthem that he sang it regularly at the lake shore whether alone or in the company of his guests. The fish in Zaca had to listen to a crackling version of "La Marseillaise" as they surfaced after an evening fly.

And then there was the Bearded Fiddler of Zaca Peak, highest and sharpest of the bastions surrounding Zaca. Gerald Drum, one of the early chroniclers of the lake, tells of hearing on his first visit the scraping notes of "The Arkansas Traveller" falling upon the smooth surface of Zaca and of seeing, high on a ledge above, an old man playing a violin tucked into the folds of a long white beard. On his second visit to the lake Drum and his two companions, tired of "scooping Indians," set off up the side of Zaca Peak to catch the fiddler, only to see him disappear into thin air as they approached his perch. In the entire literature of music no melody is more inappropriate to the perfect peace of Zaca Lake, its silent shores, its sylvan lashes than the angular collection of notes that make up the hounding tune of "The Arkansas Traveller."

Perhaps in retribution, Zaca strikes back at those of its human visitors who have looked upon it as a yielding cushion for canoes and sailboats. Many a romantic captain has set off with his admiring first mate to paddle to the center of the lake, only to discover his bark being spun in a gurgling circle by what seemed to be a giant whirlpool whose cavity reached to the very center of the earth. Helpless in this bottomless Jacuzzi, navigators of Zaca's waters have learned not to take her apparent placidity lightly, although it is now believed that lake craft are spun, not by the plumbing of the lake, but by crosswinds from deep canyons meeting and circling at its center. Drum's dream of being carried down the funnel of the whirlpool to a subterranean river and there rescued by the Bearded Fiddler at the helm of a swan-shaped boat was only a dream. Yet, the catfish and the canoes take no chances.

Then, perhaps in early spring, when the waters of Zaca have risen as much as four feet with winter rains and are spilling over into a slop basin below the lake where they form a temporary companion lake, only to leak again into clay cracks widened by summer suns, bubbles begin to rise along the shore. At first, they seem no more than beaded breath of mudcapped insects, jeweling the hem of the lake in celebration of the season. But this is no festive effervescence. As the days continue, the surface of the lake begins to change from the dark pane reflecting both inner mystery and the outer, arching canopy of greens and blues. Gradually Zaca turns to milky green, opaque and ailing, as though in a matter of hours the contents of a thousand laundromats had finally found their mark.

Zaca becomes a puddle of green milk and remains so for days. Fish, without oxygen, float to the surface forever upside down, and the smell of sulphur hovers above the surface. Gasses accumulated from plant life on the bottom, from decaying trunks of fallen trees, from the microorganisms deep in its bowels, unable to escape by the normal route of flowing water, explode in one great and silent burp.

Having cleansed itself, renewed its oxygen content, somersaulted by agonizing effort, Zaca returns again to deep clarity. Catfish, who seem to weather these upheavals by gulping surface air, survive. Lesser fish perish. Plant life as always draws nourishment from its own mortality. Until next time Zaca Lake is the innocent pond, wrinkled briefly by passing breezes. That burp you thought you noticed never really happened.

Zaca Lake, like all the Waldens of the world, faces an uncertain future in which its indigestion may be the least of its problems. For a century it has been privately owned by a succession of caretakers dedicated to leaving it alone. It is reported that once Theodore Roosevelt attempted to turn it into a national park, only to be rebuked by the singing Frenchman. Again, it was offered to the county, only to be refused by the voters as too expensive. Meanwhile, taxes rise. Like so many private places Zaca may be forced to go public. To be appreciated it must now be depreciated, which is to say that it must produce income for its owners. The lake might become a California landmark, entitling its owners to suitable assistance in preserving it. Otherwise, whether public or private, it must be populated by paying guests, and the deer and foxes and coons along its shore must withdraw, muzzles dripping, to make room for a paying species.

Thoreau believed wholeheartedly that his Walden was more than a match for woodcutters and fishermen, that each spring their traces would again be blurred by renewing nature. But the traces of modern visitors to Zaca are more permanent, and the single spring is no longer enough to renew it. Zaca, alert to its own blocked colon, has always cured itself, casting off pollution of its own making, but now, because it is there, it must pay its way. For most of nature that is not possible. It has always seemed enough that bears and oaks and eagles — and the ponds created to reflect them and to quench their thirst — were there, but lately it has not been enough. Nature too must justify her existence in the coin of one of her creations. The present owners of Zaca now pump its waters against an overhanging cliff to aerate them and to relieve those annoying gas bubbles. But as they set about the cure they calculate how many campers it will require to pay the medical costs.

Henry Thoreau wrote, "A lake is the landscape's most beautiful and expressive feature. It is earth's eye, looking into which the beholder measures the depth of his own nature." I have looked into Zaca's eye and carried home her beauty in my own.

Wouldn't You Rather Be Purple?

At the urging of a friend, whose aerie is a mountaintop in the high country which makes up my horizon, I have visited the wild flowers, and it is true that Solomon in all his glory would not compare. In draws and arroyos, on cliffsides and escarpments, over rock surfaces where even lichen would think twice, suddenly a garden is in bloom like none I have ever seen before. Color arrangements which would dazzle a decorator carpet entire hillsides, while we puny botanists below struggle to save our efforts from snails and gophers. Perfect poppies salted with popcorn flowers, Johnny jump-ups encircling lupine, scarlet sprigs of Indian paintbrush have magically appeared. To come upon one of these slanted gardens is enough to make me wonder how nature has survived all these years without Bandini.

My daughter Susie, whose habit was to read and whose gift was to remember miscellaneous information, developed a theory that the Garden of Eden was purple. In the beginning, she decided, flowers were always purple, smelled stronger and demanded attention from birds and insects. And isn't it easier, she reasoned, if you are purple, to become red or blue? Or even pink or yellow? Isn't purple the color of love? As I stood at the edge of the wild gardens cascading from the hilltop, I tested her theory. Certainly, the purple brodisea were flourishing on tall stems, inches closer to the noon sun than anything else around them. The deep blue lupin had taken over the best places and dominated the breezes. Even the smaller lobelia were doing nicely. There was no doubt that primitive purple was still strong.

But the poppies were certainly second in the contest for attention. I discovered the secret of the poppy's perfection that morning. They wear small, pointy hats right up to their entrance. Then, like a girl with a new hairdo, who keeps her head covered until it really counts, the poppies fling off their caps and unfold. Not a flaw. Not a ragged petal edge. And when the late-afternoon breeze begins to chill, the poppies fold up again. Poppies are some smart flowers.

The yellow flowers, aware of the purple menace, have solved the problem of being smelled and seen by settling in the suburbs. Fields of fiddle-necks unwind under cows' noses, safe as houses and apparently aware of it. Johnny jump-ups, which, at least while I was watching, didn't, manage to be noticeable by sticking together. And, of course, my old enemy, wild mustard, was off to a racy start this year. How many mornings I have devoted to yanking at mustard stalks in my pasture! How attractive a field filled with its yellow blossoms is when it belongs to someone else!

There were others in the wild bouquet: miner's lettuce, the salad makings for Indians and the '49'ers, owl clover with its lavender fists of blooms, fiesta flowers, blue corsages ready to cling to any surface, California lilac, no match for its eastern cousin but able to live in dry country.

So we're back to purple again. There's just no escaping the conclusion that, on the whole, it is better to be purple. Purple is the primal color. The smell of purple hangs like incense, masking more delicate perfumes, heavy on the hills. Where the wild bouquet is primitive, where time is short, soil inhospitable, rain a memory, nature still leads from strength. Purple, and its elements, blue and red, are her colors, the pennants of early spring.

Inspired, I drove to a local nursery. If the wildflowers were in bloom, certainly I could match their colors with my own, sheltered from the wind and the gophers, nursed along in redwood pots filled with planter mix and sifted soil. "To early," he told me. "Wait another month."

On that hillside at the summit, out of sight of beauty's beholder, out from under our noses, an older gardener disagreed.

The Once Again Prince

I have just accompanied an old and special horse through his final, summer-long illness, a sad and perplexing experience for us both. Horses seldom live out their lives in the familiar fields where once they felt the joy of a first spring. Their usefulness to us, and therefore their place in our lives are usually far shorter than their span of years, and even in country places where an old horse needs little attention and occupies an ever-decreasing space, we pass him along at a certain mileage, a hobby we have outgrown. A horse lasts too long for most of us. One I knew, the sire of my colt, died recently at thirty-nine. He had met his replacement on the morning of his death and his heart stopped in protest.

I say my old horse was special, and he was. Even his arrival in my field was no ordinary event. I first met Prince on a dark Thanksgiving Eve eight years ago when I returned from the city for the long weekend and went as always to feed my daughter's mare. Following a few steps behind her came a giant face out of the darkness, a head hanging like a broken branch from a crane-like neck, a concave back and a pace so slow that each step seemed painful. I had no idea how he got there, this caricature of a horse, nor where he should have been.

"It must be Prince," Jeremy told me as we left him with a wafer of hay at his feet, his great neck lowering slowly. "My riding teacher told me about him. His owners are going to sell him for dog food at next week's auction. They've even stopped feeding him."

At sunrise on Thanksgiving morning I went to the corral to look at Prince. There between me and the rising sun he was even more incongruous. His color was orange, his winter coat long and standing out from his body, his sagging back holding the ball of the new sun. His face was camel-like below a straw-colored forelock, and his eyes, even as I approached, were tightly closed, as if another morning was too much to face. Tear streaks marked crooked paths along his nose. His old eyes always watered at the downside corners. He walked when absolutely necessary with an arthritic stiffness, and his conformation by any human measure of horse beauty was hopelessly wrong.

Over the long weekend my daughter Jeremy and I fed and groomed Prince with gentle hands he seemed to enjoy. He accepted his first carrot, his private pile of hay with cautious disbelief. We called our blacksmith who advised shoes on his front hooves to even out his sloping posture and to relieve the painful tilt caused by too much weight in front. With new front shoes Prince stood as might a little girl showing off her shiny patent leathers, his hooves touching and carefully aligned. Even being shod he shut his eyes. Nothing seemed to matter.

Of course, we could not keep a stolen horse. Nor could we return him to owners prepared to sell him by the pound. I called the woman who had hidden Prince in our field, asked her to find out what price he would have brought from bidders representing dog food companies, scavengers always present at the close of every sale to buy for bargain prices the leftovers. The answer came quickly. Prince's price was one hundred twelve dollars.

At the end of Jeremy's Saturday riding lesson I gave a check to her teacher. I never knew nor wanted to know the identity of Prince's owners. The following week I met two friends for lunch, men I worked with in the music business. I told them the story of my rustled horse and the ransom I had paid. My friends were city men, never closer to a horse than the paddock at Santa Anita, but both insisted they must own a share of my orange horse. Each gave me a check for one third of Prince, returning to their offices proud part owners of a horse they would never see.

As the winter weeks passed, Prince began to change. Doggedly he followed Jeremy's mare up and down the pasture, deeply in love. Now his eyes were open, russet pools in his barren, homely face. Now he stepped a little faster to keep up. He suffered a saddle which filled the hollow of his back, leveling out his profile. He still looked like a huge, shaggy toy, a horse exaggerated for a laugh, but he held his head higher, he swished his tail as if it mattered, and the rows of his ribs, which once had corduroyed his flanks, began to disappear.

In March our mare gave birth to a pure white colt in a drenching rain. It was our first-born horse, a memorable event for my daughter and me, but a much more satisfying one for Prince. Although gelded, Prince was certain the colt was his, and fatherhood became the final miracle. His courting days were over. Now he led the mare, guided the wobbling colt, and walked tall. It was he who chose their path, the patch of shade at noon, the green puddle of burr clover. He also found his voice, a deep ahem, and at meal times he rattled the aluminum gate with one shoe, impatient if we were late.

As his adopted son grew strong and challenging, Prince took over his discipline, never bothering to chase him, for nothing was worth the hurry, but administering necessary nips along the way. There was no longer any doubt that he had been properly named long ago when someone's hopes for him were high. At the far end of the pasture there is an auxiliary water trough the size and depth of a bathtub. After sucking his fill from this small trough, Prince would step carefully into it to stand for hours with both front feet in the water. His family could drink elsewhere. As the days of spring penetrated and warmed, his winter coat fell away in tufts, each to be carried off to line the nests of larks and red-wing blackbirds. He put up with little girls straddling his scooped-out back and now and then would carry them a few steps before stopping to close his eyes.

And so he lived, a once again Prince, his self respect restored, his days of ignominy long forgotten. He suffered Saturday shampoos, standing in a cloud of suds, feeling the squirt of the hose, drying off by noon. He stood long hours at the fence corner gazing off toward the mountains, then resting his chin on a fence post to nap. Caught for a moment each evening between me and the setting sun, he seemed a golden horse, a misshapen Pegasus pausing between heavenly adventures.

I returned early this summer from an eastern trip to find Prince noticeably thinner. Tests revealed the presence of worms which were quickly eliminated, but his weight continued to drop. A rich diet of mixed grains and molasses was added, served three times a day in a bread pan to fit his jaws. Still he shrunk before my eyes, his ribs reappearing, the sag of his back emphasizing the emerging crags of his quarters. He still walked toward me, but he allowed me to do most of the walking, and he chewed each mouthful with less and less enthusiasm. The pill he now took once a day, powdered and mixed with his grain, had no effect. New tests of blood and liver revealed no malfunction, but nothing helped. He spent his days in deep grass seldom reaching down to graze, and more and more I saw his eyes turned toward the mountains far away. I spoke quietly at such times, reminding him how fortunate we both were, reassuring him that all would be well. He, as I, knew better.

This slow withdrawal continued over three months. The great orange horse was fading before my eyes, and nothing I did made any difference. His mare and colt stayed near, but they seemed forgotten. He seemed already to have left them. He turned often to stare behind him, puzzled by the failure far back. His tear streaks lengthened, and as I dried them with my sleeve to keep the flies away, he bowed his head to allow me to scratch his forelock.

On a morning in mid-October Prince returned to the corral and lay down at last. By then he was the shadow horse I had seen long ago. He could not raise his head to nibble at the sweet-smelling breakfast I brought, and I called John, my friend and veterinarian, who skipped his own breakfast to come to us. There in the corral Prince went to sleep. It was all we could do for him, a gentle push toward the mountains he now could climb.

It is not possible here at the end of summer to bury a great animal in the cementlike adobe packed by hooves for rainless months. There is only one solution, difficult to face. John called the only horse hearse available, a great, iron-clad truck which roams the valley keeping in touch by radio with daily tragedies like mine. Before noon the ugly vehicle rolled in, driven by an old man with a cheerful Santa Claus face. The only feature of this chariot to identify its purpose was a high crane and a winch wound with steel cable.

"Do you need me?" I asked the driver, pointing to the corral.

"You stay here," he said, all rosy and smiling. "I've been doing this for forty-three years."

He was there no more than ten minutes. As he pulled away from the gate, the high gray siding of the truck hiding its cargo, I called to thank him. He waved, and an old dog appeared beside him in the truck seat. "My dog's blind," he called. "Maybe it's just as well."

We who choose to surround ourselves with lives even more temporary than our own live within a fragile circle, easily and often breached. Unable to accept its awful gaps, we still would live no other way. We cherish memory as the only certain immortality, never fully understanding the necessary plan. The life of a horse, often half our own, seems endless until one day. That day has come and gone for me, and I am once again within a somewhat smaller circle, still unable to believe that this evening I will not see Prince within the setting sun, head lowered, eyes half closed, tail a golden fall.

He was and is again a Prince to us. I hope he stands proud always, his two new shoes held tight together until it is time to rattle another gate. His summons will not go unheeded.